A Forest Aflame

Seventy-Five Years
at
Epworth Forest

by John N. Elliott
and Joyce W. Elliott

Fairway Press, Lima, Ohio

A FOREST AFLAME

Written by
John N. Elliott
Joyce W. Elliott

FIRST EDITION
Copyright © 2000 by
Epworth Forest Conference Center

ISBN 0-7880-1636-9   PRINTED IN U.S.A.

A Word Of
Appreciation And Thanks

John and Joyce Elliott have been our dear friends for more than thirty years. So it is with great pleasure that I write these words of deep appreciation for their willingness to undertake the daunting task of writing this book. Before writing, countless days of research, involving both oral interviews and written records, had to be done. An interesting format stressing life-changing stories experienced at Epworth Forest also had to be designed. All of this took not only time and energy, but also great devotion to a most difficult task, one to be completed cooperatively by two very busy persons.

This has been a venture of faith. FALEF (Friends and Alumni of Epworth Forest) Board encouraged and authorized the book but could only pay expenses — no honorarium! So it has been a labor of love! John and Joyce, we thank you for a job well done. Also, our thanks to Shane Hartman, Executive Director of Epworth Forest Conference Center, for his cooperation and support.

Now a word of challenge. Over a three-year period (1997-2000) FALEF brought about the beautiful renovation of Freeland House at a savings of over $300,000 to our Annual Conference. Over 200 volunteers — adults and youth — accomplished this!

FALEF is basically the "Alumni Association" of Epworth Forest. We seek to do all we can to beautify and improve the buildings and grounds. These are sacred grounds! [The mission of FALEF is to strengthen and enhance the ministry of Epworth Forest C.C. through remembering God's touch, sharing our enthusiasm, encouraging positive relationships, and mobilizing resources.]

We challenge each of you to join us in FALEF as we serve together to ensure that the life-changing ministries of Epworth Forest C.C. will continue with growing strength and vitality in this new 21st century.

Rev. Bob Glass
President of FALEF

P.S. To become a member of FALEF simply call Epworth Forest C.C. Our Annual Meeting is always the Saturday noon of Choir School, August 5, 2000. Come and join us.

Please send your membership to: Epworth Forest Conference Center, North Webster, Indiana 46555.

Table Of Contents

Foreword

This is the third history of Epworth Forest. It covers the 25 years from 1974 through 1999 and has a different focus from that of its predecessors.

In 1949 Rev. William B. Freeland wrote *Epworth Forest, The First 25 Years*. In that first history, Rev. Freeland carefully chronicled the development of the camp from its earliest beginnings in 1924.

Twenty-five years later Rev. Orrin Manifold described the quarter century, 1949-1974, in *Epworth Forest, The First Fifty Years*. His book included a reprint of Freeland's book.

Both volumes faithfully reflected the changing spirit and issues of their times. This third volume also mirrors many changes — changes which some can embrace but others may decry.

Both earlier volumes documented the history of the camp by focusing on the hard work and crucial decisions made by pivotal leaders, committees, and boards — the *business* end of Epworth Forest, if you will. But the current writers believe that the most significant portrait of Epworth Forest has not yet been painted. And so this volume is different.

When the opportunity to write this book was first offered by the Friends and Alumni of Epworth Forest (FALEF), we began to pray and reflect on how best to document the true impact of Epworth Forest. Immediately we were reminded of our own holy experiences at the camp and the miracle of changed lives experienced by so many others who have walked its grounds.

It is those stories of transformed lives, we concluded, that paint the most significant portrait of the camp. For Epworth Forest is more than a wooded campground. It is, and has been since its beginning, *A Forest Aflame* with the Holy Spirit. And through the lives it has transformed, that Spirit has spread to some of the farthest reaches of the globe and impacted many areas of life, both secular and sacred. That is no small accomplishment for any institution. Clearly, it is an accomplishment that merits humble and grateful recounting, insofar as that is possible.

This different focus on the history of Epworth Forest is in no way meant to denigrate the sacrificial and visionary work of those who so faithfully attended to the business end of life at Epworth Forest. Nor is it intended to diminish the careful, even painstaking documentation done by Reverends Freeland and Manifold. But just as their books reflected changes in their times, perhaps this one reflects a heightened spiritual awareness in ours.

We realize that God's saving grace and wondrous ways can never fully be described in words. God's actions are customarily filled with mystery whenever they are perceived. But God has always blessed sincere efforts to witness to Him. So we trust God to bless our efforts to witness to what He has done in the secret chambers of many hearts.

Finding the stories ...

Once FALEF had granted permission to write the present history with this new focus, we set about the job of finding appropriate sources for stories. Although we knew there were many, many stories of transformed lives to be found, the challenge of actually tracking them down proved to be a big one. In an effort not to overlook any area of life at Epworth Forest that might produce such stories, we plunged deep into Conference minutes and other written records at the Conference office and at the Epworth Forest and Camp Adventure campgrounds. To our dismay, we found that in too many cases the needed records were here, there, and nowhere.

Nevertheless, using the information we could glean from those sources, we wrote scores of letters, made countless phone calls, and traveled many miles in pursuit of interviews that would reveal stories of transformed lives.

Some of the people interviewed quickly recounted such stories — so vivid was their memory of them. Others claimed initially they had no special story to tell. However, after a few minutes of reminiscing, the floodgates would often open, and their heart's most precious treasures would pour forth. We were deeply enriched by many of those stories and thank God for the opportunity to hear and record them.

In the end, despite the fact that many of our letters and phone calls went unanswered, we ended up with a body of stories far too extensive to include in its entirety here. For the omissions we sincerely apologize. All interviews, both in their taped and transcribed forms, will be submitted to the Methodist archives at DePauw University once this volume is published. So none is actually lost.

We are fully aware that the stories in this volume are but the slender peak of the mighty mountain of work God continues to do at Epworth Forest. We pray God will bless those whose accounts are found in these pages as well as those who read and honor them. And we hope these pages may be used by God to continue to bless the *forest aflame* that is nestled along the north shore of beautiful Lake Webster in northern Indiana.

John and Joyce Elliott
2/2000

The Impact Of Merger

Although the official span of this book is the quarter century from 1974 through 1999, in truth it extends backward to include the years from 1968 onward. The reason: The merger between the Evangelical United Brethren Church and The Methodist Church which occurred in 1968 started "a dizzying series of changes in structure and relationship," (*Epworth Forest, The First Fifty Years*, O. W. Manifold). Many of those changes directly impacted the camping program across Indiana.

When the merger dust of 1968 settled, the newly organized North Indiana Conference owned seven campgrounds! Each camp had its own traditions, clientele, leadership styles, and funding process. Confusion prevailed. General Conference drew up a "simplified" restructuring of the camping program in 1968 only to have the General Conference of 1972 change it.

And other changes have ensued. Those changes, together with an unbelievable proliferation and diversification of programs at Epworth Forest, have made a detailed, chronological documentation of post-merger events impractical, if not impossible. (NOTE: There is a very brief chronology of some events on pages 66-74 of this book.)

All this is stated as a sort of caveat to those who, having read the two previous histories, might tend to expect more of the same in this one. Not so. The 1968 merger was a watershed into a whole new era of life for Methodist institutions everywhere. Epworth Forest was no exception.

Positive Signs Of The Times — Major Trends

Records of life at Epworth Forest over the years since Merger reveal three major trends. We call these positive signs of the times because to us they bear witness to an intentional effort to make the camp contemporary and responsible in the best sense of the words.

One trend is the burgeoning of programs and events. Epworth Forest and Camp Adventure now host an amazing variety of camps, conferences, retreats, rallies, seminars, and other gatherings. In doing so they fill a wide spectrum of needs for people in many walks of life. From Elderhostels to youth camps to fitness seminars and beyond: That has become the scope of life at Epworth Forest.

Another trend is an increasing commitment to excellence. Programs and events at Epworth Forest are increasingly well planned, carefully evaluated, and improved. Thousands of man hours, tons of paper, and stacks of computer disks bear witness to this trend.

Yet another trend is the proliferation of effective and ever more appealing promotional materials and media. Note the cover for this book as an example. And another: the Board of Camps and Conferences now has a web site: www.extremecamp.org. Although the site may not be for the fainthearted over fifty, the youth love it. What is more, they use it! Assuredly, it is responsible, in part at least, for the fact that 1998 and 1999 saw the number of youth campers jump by a whopping 33%. That's an increase of over 1,000 campers in two years!

It is against this backdrop of post-merger developments, then, that this current history is written. But in order truly to set the last twenty-five or so years in perspective, in order to make this a true celebration of seventy-five years at Epworth Forest, we need to recall some of our earlier history as well. We have taken the liberty of doing so by recalling stories and events of earlier times that catch the flavor of this fine institution as it has evolved through the past three-quarters of a century.

John and Joyce Elliott
2/2000

Chapter I

The Uniqueness Of Epworth Forest

It was not long after merger that Epworth Forest began to be recognized as a truly unique campground. A committee set up to survey and evaluate the seven North Indiana Conference campgrounds found it quite unlike any of the others.

Perhaps its greatest uniqueness lay in the fact that it was the only one of the seven camps where church-owned cottages, not dorms, provided the primary living units for youth campers. (It was to become the largest Christian conference center in Indiana and, for some years it was the largest Senior High Institute Program in the U. S. A.) In addition, the intimacy of cottage living was well integrated with the life of the greater campground.

Bishop Sheldon Duecker, states, "I have not seen anything like Epworth Forest being reproduced anywhere else in this country."

In the end its uniqueness, its facilities, and the high quality of programming it offered saved Epworth Forest from being sold. Not all of the other six campgrounds were so spared.

But the uniqueness of Epworth Forest has long extended beyond its living arrangements, its facilities, and its programming. There is a feeling of community on the campground that makes it very special. It is a "coming home" place for many, offering love, security, and spiritual nurture. The people who live there, both seasonally and year-round, often become part of a bigger family. A kind of spiritual bonding often occurs within that bigger family.

True, in recent years, the Epworth Forest family has become more diversified than in previous years. The campground is no longer the homogeneous haven of Methodists it once was. People of other denominations and no denominations at all have bought properties there. People with a wide variety of lifestyles have moved in. Sometimes there have been dramatic differences of opinion over property rights and responsibilities. But the bonding of residents still occurs.

Here's an example of that bonding:

Cookie Man

Cottage resident Bill Beuoy had a neighbor who had been a recovering alcoholic for eight years. Except for language that was often heavily peppered with swear words, this man seemed agreeable enough, a bit rough, and apparently not a churchgoer, but agreeable enough.

About two years previous to the time of this story, however, this man's mother died, and he was so devastated by her death that he went back to drinking. Soon thereafter he lost his job; and, following a drinking binge, ended up in jail. While there he fell and broke some ribs.

When the man was released from jail, he invited Bill over to his cottage, where he immediately began offering some of his home furnishings for sale. Puzzled, Bill refused the offers politely. Finally, the man leveled with him: he was broke and needed money for food.

Bill told him that he would not buy anything, but he would give him a job if he wanted one, once the man's ribs were healed. There was just one stipulation: if the man were to work for Bill, he was to refrain from swearing *and* from drinking.

Apparently the man made no commitment at that time.

Some months later, during devotions one morning, Bill felt "under conviction" to talk to the man again. Several older residents of the campground had been hiring Bill to put their piers into the lake, and he definitely could use some help.

By that time the man's ribs were healed, and his drinking problem was under control again. He agreed to help Bill with the piers.

Conversation with the man was a bit difficult at first. Many a sentence ended up half finished as the man struggled to eliminate the more colorful words from his vocabulary. Slowly, however, he managed to do that, and the two men got better and better acquainted.

One day Bill began to talk about his church and what it meant to him. The man became more and more interested as the weeks went by. Finally, quite out of the blue, he asked Bill if there was anything he might do for that church.

"Well, we can always use cookies for the social hour," Bill answered, half joking.

"Man, I love to bake cookies!" was the man's instant reply.

And from that day on he became known as "the cookie man" in Bill's church.

He and his wife eventually joined that church, and he ultimately became its lay leader as well as a delegate to Annual Conference.

Such are the fruits of bonding at Epworth Forest.

Story told by Tom Frost.

"Epworth Forest is a living shrine," says Bishop Duecker, and this certainly does seem to be the feeling of many. For some people, there are even particular "holy" places on the grounds. The late John Dicken had his special "meditation tree." The old fountain was special to others, the lakeshore to many. The auditorium ... the amphitheater ... the chapel ... the Christ statue. And the list goes on.

Even for those not privileged to participate much in the life of Epworth Forest, the campground sometimes holds a special place in the heart. Carl Erskine, the one-time ace pitcher for the Brooklyn Dodgers, bears witness to that fact. Erskine was once a special speaker at Institute, but this particular story comes from earlier in his life:

As a youth, Erskine often visited a cottage on the opposite shore of Lake Webster. It was the Lowell Palmer cottage, the summer home of his childhood sweetheart and future wife. Boating and fishing on the lake were common pastimes for Erskine and his future father-in-law, and one Sunday morning that pastime brought a very special experience.

A Calm Lake and Pealing Bells

"It was early morning," Erskine relates. Lowell was rowing and I was sitting in the front of the boat watching the bow slice

3

through the perfectly calm water and sort of parting the overhanging fog. It felt like one of those pictures of heaven where the clouds are floating around.

"Suddenly over this wonderful quiet came these bells pealing across the lake from Epworth Forest, their chimes playing 'All Hail the Power of Jesus' Name.' I want to tell you, as a teenager that simple experience had a huge, huge impact on me.

"Later on when I was with the Dodgers, whenever I would get tense and feel my muscles too strained, I learned to close my eyes, literally, and envision the shore of Lake Webster, the calm water, the peaceful fog, and the chimes playing 'All Hail the Power of Jesus' Name.' It relaxed me every time.

"And to this day, whenever I hear that hymn, the experience of peace and calm returns as well as my personal inner picture of that morning and those bells at Epworth Forest."

Carl Erskine

Note: Dr. Norman Vincent Peale later referred to this incident in his writings.

The Forest is aflame in the community of Epworth Forest.

Chapter 2

Institute

W. B. Freeland gives credit for the name "Institute" to Rev. Thomas Nicholson, one-time Secretary of the Board of Education and later bishop of the Methodist Episcopal Church

Sometime in the early decades of last century Nicholson suggested "the Institute Plan — a simple organization for a summer assembly with appropriate officers to plan and conduct it." The plan included a faculty of college professors, ministers, missionaries and additional leaders skilled in athletics and entertainment.

When first tried, the Institute model shocked some stern and staid Methodists. Apparently they were skeptical that any mix of youthful energy and "horseplay" with courses on Bible, missions, and social services would work. But work it did. And soon it became obvious that Institute was here to stay.

Though greatly changed from its beginnings, Institute has long been the centerpiece of life at Epworth Forest, involving the greatest number of participants of any program offered there.

True, the days when hundreds of youth from a single district crowded the campground each week are gone. But we must realize that those were the days before drivers education, summer school, band camps, cheerleading camps, athletic camps, and summer jobs became such an big part of teen life.

Now, of course, it is common practice for youth from two or more districts to share a week at Institute. But it still remains far and away the largest camping program in the North Indiana Conference. Indeed, few camping programs in the nation are as large; even fewer have a similar program.

For those unfamiliar with Institute at Epworth Forest, perhaps a brief description is in order:

First of all, there are the living arrangements. Youth from each church live together, eat together, do chores together, have evening devotions together, and sleep together in the same cottage. This togetherness is both intense and intentional and has been a prized Institute tradition for decades. Pastors have found that it not only enriches camp life during Institute week but also strengthens youth programs in the local church. It develops a level of group trust and confidence difficult to come by in any other way.

"As a young pastor I learned that one week at Epworth Forest had more impact on the lives of our youth than fifty-two U. M. Y. F. Sunday night meetings in the local church," Rev. Jack Pavy once said.

Second, there are the facilities available. These include a swimming beach, a large auditorium, a gift shop, a snack bar, a boating harbor for sailboats and canoes, hiking trails, tennis courts, basketball and volleyball courts, soccer fields, softball diamonds, and horseshoe pits.

Third, there is the dedicated support staff, which ranges all the way from deans and keynoters to cottage cooks and counselors to supervisors of each of the above facilities to office workers to grounds keepers and garbage collectors.

Fourth, there are the activities offered. Each week a carefully chosen spiritual theme is introduced and developed by a carefully chosen Keynoter. Each theme is designed to inspire discussion in small response groups that meet daily with leaders who have been well supplied with resource materials weeks earlier. Worship services, prayer groups, drama presentations, concerts by Christian groups, special interest workshops, a variety of athletic activities, and free time — all are a part of life at Institute.

All the above only begin to describe the "draw" of Institute. Perhaps Rev. Marc Blaising describes that "draw" best:

"(Institute) is a place of *focused activity* from dawn until late at night. We know why we are there — to pray and to talk with God, to learn more abut Jesus and what it means to follow him."

"(Institute) is also a place of *decision*.. Literally hundreds have made personal decisions to accept Jesus as the Christ and as their Lord and Savior there.

(Institute) also means *service*. The decisions made there are to be acted out."

The key words here are decision and service. Every Institute week has its Commitment or Decision Night — a night wherein youth are invited (but not pressured) to make a decision to invite Christ into their lives or to serve him in one way or another. It is the spiritual highlight of the week, and it is taken very seriously.

As Bishop Sheldon Duecker once pointed out, for many youth Institute may be the only place where they are expected to be accountable in a spiritual way. Small wonder, then, that it has impacted so many hundreds of lives.

There is such an abundance of stories of lives positively impacted by experiences at Institute! Let us share some:

Calls to Ministry

"Epworth Forest is holy ground for me. My call to ordained ministry actually came during the summer after my sophomore year in high school, but I convinced myself that any sense of 'call' was really just the emotions of the week, and I did not respond on Decision Night that year.

"However, the following year my sense of being called into ordained ministry was very strong all week at Institute, and so I did go forward during the Friday night service. I still remember the wide range of emotions that I felt: fear, relief, joy, excitement, and confusion.

"... I talked at length that evening with our youth pastor, Rev. Bill Mathys, and by the next morning I was ready to sing the Doxology with a strong sense of assurance that I was, indeed, responding to God's call in my life.

"In later years I served as Institute Keynoter three times and (on Decision Nights) I vividly remember thinking, 'So this is what it feels like to be on the other side of the invitation.' For me it was just as emotional to issue the call as it had been to respond to it years before."

Michael J. Coyner

"Over 50 years ago, in July of 1948, I attended the Ft. Wayne District Institute. My steady girlfriend came with me. I had just graduated from high school. I was headed for college, though I hadn't made any career plans yet. World War II was a fading memory. Jitterbugging was all the rage. Life was good, and I had the world by the tail.

"Having attended camps at Epworth Forest since seventh grade, I knew the drill. This was to be my fourth and final Institute, and I knew what to expect, or thought I did.

"The week progressed pretty much as Institute weeks in previous years had, though I don't remember many of the details. I do remember that we Instituters beat the preachers in the end-of-the-week softball game — a sweet victory.

"On Commitment night, I sat in the back row of the auditorium with my girl. I had no intention of responding to Rev. Donald Bailey's challenge to ... anything.

"Then why did I suddenly find myself standing up, stepping into the aisle, and heading toward the front of the auditorium when his call for full-time Christian service came?

"In one sense I knew exactly what was happening, but in another sense I was strangely out of control. It was my first major, honest-to-God mystery. I was convinced, however, that I was doing what I had to do, going where I had to go.

"Afterward, when some pastor — I can't remember who — took me to a quiet place to talk, I remember exactly what I told him: I definitely felt called to full-time Christian service but I would *not* be a missionary and I would *not* be a pastor. Maybe I'd be a Christian lawyer ... or some-thing.

"As things turned out, I was wrong on all three counts. God's Spirit led me first to the mission field in India and then to pastorates in North Indiana. God not only took care of my career plans but of my entire life — all on one fateful night in July, 1948. How profoundly grateful I am for that one night! My life has never been the same since."

John Elliott

"I did not experience lightning and thunder in accepting Christ or in being called into full-time ministry at Institute. I never heard

8

God's voice speaking to me. For many years I wondered why anyone would want to hear the story of how I came into the ministry. But perhaps there are others who need to hear how God deals with people in many different ways.

"God took me where I was — a shy, insecure boy with low self-esteem who came from a broken home. God worked with me in slow, steady, and progressive ways. I can see that now.

"I would never have come to Institute; never. Nor to Boyville or to Camp Adventure if my local church had not encouraged and supported me!

"I grew up just a half-block from that church. My family certainly didn't belong to those fine folks, but they took us in. I was one of them from cradle roll through college but only because they loved and nurtured me my whole growing-up life.

"It took me several years of Decision Nights at Institute finally to acknowledge and accept God's call to Christian ministry. It didn't happen until my final year, when I had just graduated from high school. In retrospect I think I must have known I could not come back again to Institute. It was my last chance to accept God's call, and I did.

"I thank God that Epworth Forest was there for me and for hundreds of other young people."

Jay Morris

Commitments to Christ

"My very first time at Institute, I was the only youth from our church who attended. I joined my cousin's group from another Methodist church.

"When the call came for commitment late in the week, I could not have remained in my seat — there was no way I could! The call was very clear; there was just absolutely no question. It wouldn't have mattered who was around me, I had to step out."

Rosemary Manifold

"My most precious memory of Epworth Forest was the evening I accepted Christ during the Friday night communion. I had played

9

the organ for 'Oh, so many,' communion services swatting millions of mosquitoes and witnessing about every kind of bug buzzing near the organ light.

"That summer, after my sophomore year in high school, I was asked to be a real Instituter by Kokomo Beamer Church. I attended classes and I lived with the Beamer bunch in Parkview Cottage.

"It was a week, including squirt-gun fights, kitchen duty, and then meaningful devotions, morning watch, and then Friday night when my spiritual life was changed. That night I didn't play the organ — I was a real camper and became a real Christian."

Rebecca Chance Carrington

The files at Epworth Forest are filled with statistics of commitments like the ones above as well as many other kinds of commitments — first-time commitments to accept Christ as Lord and Savior, recommitments to accept Christ as Lord and Savior, and the list goes on. Those are heartening statistics, to be sure.

But what about the Spirit-filled experiences that never become statistics? What about the quiet, profound touches of God that occur during sharing times in cottages, during quiet strolls along the beach, or during some late night vigil in the chapel?

Here are accounts of some of those experiences:

Strength and the Holy Spirit

"At Institute I could feel God, the love warming us ... especially in evenings when we had prayer and share and knew it was confidential.

"(At night) looking up at the stars would light a little fire within me, and I'd go home on fire for God.

"Institute gave me a kind of inspiration. It was like God telling me, 'It's all right. You can still go on. I'm giving you this place and time to keep you going.' "

Jenny Mabry

"I attended a South Bend Institute where, on one particular day, the Holy Spirit filled the entire grounds. It was the most amazing experience — hours of singing, running hand-in-hand, lakeside baptisms — all spontaneous.

"The love of God and a sense of His presence was so real and powerful that even the rocks and trees must have had the urge to cry out with joy!

"I've often wondered what initiated it. The Keynoter? A testimony? The singing group? I sure can't remember.

"I can say, however, that I've never experienced such an outpouring of God's Spirit on hundreds of people as on that day. Wow!"

Ed Fenstermacher

Turning Points

"One year while I was Keynoter at Institute two sisters came to see me in our cottage. The 17-year-old brought her younger sister because that sister was having a terrible time with their parents.

"We talked for a while and I asked a few questions. The younger sister finally began to level with me. She confessed she was into drugs and was having an affair with an older man. She said she would sneak out at night to meet this man and then lie about it to her parents afterward.

"After owning up to all this mess, the girl asked me, 'Well, what do you think?'

"I was praying hard, but I decided I had to be honest. "Well," I said, "if I were your parents, I wouldn't trust you either."

"The girl began to sob uncontrollably. I held her close and asked,

" 'Have you ever thought of trying it the other way?'

" 'How? What other way?'

" 'No lies; no drugs; no affair! The way you are living is not God's dream for you,' I said.

"Then I explained how much God loved her. But I could not tell whether she believed me or not.

"Institute ended. I didn't hear from the girls again for the rest of that week.

"Some months later I was invited to speak at a banquet in the Calumet District. I was amazed to find those two sisters serving as greeters. But that wasn't the biggest amazement of the evening.

11

"After the program a neat couple came up to me and said, 'We don't know what happened at Institute, but our youngest daughter has undergone a complete about-face since then! It's just unbelievable! If you had anything to do with it, we cannot thank you enough.'

"I felt so blessed! When I told the girl at my cottage that if I were her parent, I wouldn't be able to trust her, I was so afraid it was the wrong thing to say. God had to be helping both of us. I believe honesty with love rather than honesty as judgment made the difference."

Anita Fenstermacher

"One year a young man came (to Institute) who was definitely not accepted by the other youth from our church. He was different, even strange. His words and actions embarrassed the other youth constantly. They didn't even want to be around him.

"Each day the group spent an hour after lunch interacting with the pastor and with each other. I will never forget the hour when that young man spoke out.

"Apparently the climate was such that he felt free to tell his story that day. So he explained to us how his brain had been damaged at birth. He described daily experiences of being considered weird by all his peers and even by his family. He shared how it felt to be separated from everyone else, never to fit in, to be completely alone in the world.

"Well, when he finished his story, there wasn't a dry eye in our cottage. After that hour every young person in our group accepted that young man and affirmed him just as he was.... His story was a transforming experience for everyone who was there, including myself.

"God had given him the strength to pour out his heart to us, and as we listened, God had touched all of us. It was a wonderful example of the renewing power of true confession, reconciliation, and rebirth."

Sheldon Duecker

"One year our cottage was asked to make room for a young man from a severely dysfunctional family — a boy filled with hurt and anger and feeling abandoned by just about everyone.

"The youth in our group knew and liked each other. They were a solid group, prepared for a good Institute but definitely not prepared for a troubled, disruptive young man in their midst — one who did not belong at all.

"It certainly was a challenge to have him with us, but we all made a real effort to show him love and acceptance and understanding.

"At first that effort seemed fruitless. But then bit by bit the young man began to respond more positively.

"The group grew in their understanding of Christian discipleship through the challenges of that week. Before it was over we all prayed together that this young man's life would be better.

"That prayer and our love effected one of the most dramatic changes I have ever seen. The young man made peace with his life in so many ways before going home. And we all felt blessed."

Peggy Arter Good

"One special boy arrived at Institute one Sunday afternoon alone and lonely. One wonders where they come from and what brings them to Institute. Some boys and girls seem to have no visible means of emotional support. No friends, youth or adult ... They hang around the fringes, more observers than participants. It often takes considerable effort and dedication to budge them from the fringes, to get them to participate in anything.

"This particular youth was definitely a fringe hanger, an observer. To the best of anyone's knowledge, he really did not have any friends.

"That first evening, however, things began to change. The Keynoter said something that gave him a sense of worth and reassurance unlike any he had ever heard. Somehow the undeniable conviction that God loved HIM, even him, reached him with a power that penetrated his loneliness.

"He visited the Keynoter the following noon and every noon through the week. Noontime by noontime the boy unburdened himself, breaking the Keynoter's heart day by day.

"For she learned that here was a boy who had come to Institute with the steadfast, longstanding conviction that he was unloveable. Totally unworthy of *anybody's* love — that's how he saw himself. And for good reason: He could never remember being loved by anyone. Even his mother refused to show him the slightest affection. He had convinced himself early in life that if nobody loved him, he must certainly be unloveable.

"Each day the Keynoter painstakingly reassured him that even if no human had ever loved him, God loved him and always has. Slowly the boy's conviction of unloveableness began to melt away.

"On the last day of Institute, while everybody else was packing and preparing to leave, the boy made a final visit to the Keynoter.

" 'You know what?' he asked. 'For the very first time in my life, I actually feel *loved*. I figure if God really loves me, as you say he does, then I can't possibly be unloveable.'

" 'You got that right,' the Keynoter said as she hugged him tight.

"That boy left Institute with a wonderful new sense of dignity, self-worth, yes, and belonging. He may not have made any other friends that week, but he had gotten well acquainted with the best friend of all, Jesus Christ."

Anita Fenstermacher

"I remember one Institute in particular because of one of the girls in my response group.

"I knew this young lady was having a particularly difficult time. She came from a broken home. We all knew she was having trouble with her stepmother. She had shared that quite openly.

"On the last day of Institute I asked each group member what he or she needed in order to go back home and enter the real world. As each one knelt and shared, we formed a circle around that person, laid our hands on them, and prayed that God would give them what they needed to face life at home.

"The young lady in question expressed a deep concern about going home. She asked us to pray especially hard for her. She knelt in our circle, and we all laid hands on her head and shoulders and prayed.

"I was pleased that every person took part, not only in sharing needs but also in laying hands on the others and praying.

"After all the others had left, the young lady came to me and said, 'Now I can go home to my family and not do what I was going to do. I have hated my stepmother so much that I had every intention of killing her. I had all the details worked out. But now I can go home, and I know I won't do that.'

"And she didn't."

Leroy Wise

Impact on Families

Institute is not just for high school youth. Families get involved, too, sometimes — especially the families of the pastors who attend. Although Institute is not designed primarily for them, God often touches them as richly as others:

"I will never forget that at Wednesday's Mission Night the very first year I took youth to Institute, our Kathie, a fifth-grader,was so challenged that she pledged one-half of her allowance for the entire next year to the project the missionary described."

Jack Pavy

"The year I was Keynoter at Institute — 1983 — our planning team erected a large cross on the stage of the auditorium as part of the week's unique rendering of Commitment/Covenant of Silence Night.

"As the Commitment Night worship closed, I sent the youth back to their cottages with this special invitation:

"After writing a covenant promise between themselves and God, they were free to return to the auditorium and nail their covenants to the cross.

"Lee Anne, my wife, was with our children during the Covenant of Silence back at our cottage. My oldest daughter, Gina, age six, asked her mom, 'What are these boys and girls doing?' Lee Anne said, 'Some of them are asking God to forgive them, some are making promises, and others are asking Jesus into their hearts.'

"Gina responded, 'I want to ask Jesus into my heart, too.' And while she and her mother were working on her commitments, Kelly, age four, chimed in, 'Me, too!'

"Later, Lee Anne took Gina and Kelly to the auditorium, and I met them there. As their three commitments got nailed to the cross, our family shared a very special moment, indeed.

"I know the girls have made new commitments and renewed them over and over in the intervening years, but their walk with Christ really began in a personal way there at that old cross, gathered with their mom and dad and some senior high youth."

Herb Buwalda

"As a small child, I recall running down to Lake Webster in my bathing suit, peeking in at my dad through his office window on the way.

"(Years later) I finally had the opportunity to participate more regularly in Institute and other parts of Epworth Forest life.

"Ironically, it is not so much the structured events that stand out in memory.... What makes Epworth Forest a special place for me is that I have seemingly always sensed that it is a holy place, that I am on sacred ground there, in sacred space.

"Of course that sense of holiness had been planted in me by those structured experiences.... Even though the specific people and events are blurred in memory, their purpose became reality for me. They imparted to me some sense of who God is and what my calling might be.

"Now the roots they nurtured help keep me grounded, wherever I am, as I live out the calling I began to feel so long ago, at Epworth Forest."

Bonnie Glass MacDonald

Christian Drama

The inception of Christian drama at Institute was largely the result of the determined efforts of Reverend Charles (Chuck) Johnson. Chuck's longtime involvement with drama had given him a deep appreciation of the medium as a worthy and unique venue for instruction. He worked hard to win a place for Christian drama at Institute.

Chuck's efforts paid off in 1967, when Dr. Alfred Edyvean of Christian Theological Seminary in Indianapolis was invited to bring his drama troupe to Institute. Dr. Edyvean directed dramatic performances at Institute for the next two decades.

The makeup and size of the Edyvean drama troupe was different each year. It was not unusual to have as many as ten student actors receiving stipends and another ten high school apprentices in the troupe.

Toward the end of the 1980s, as budget constraints became tighter, leaders at Institute were forced to look for places to save money. Ultimately it was decided to replace the Edyvean group with the Covenant Players, who used fewer actors in their presentations. Today drama is presented at Institute by groups from the University of Indianapolis.

The inception of drama at Institute marked an important new direction in instruction there. And it was not always without its detractors. However, over time, the effectiveness and high quality of the presentations generated more and more positive response. Eventually the performances not only drew crowds of Epworth Forest residents but also people from the town of North Webster and surrounding areas. Sometimes the auditorium doors were kept closed until all Instituters had been seated just to make sure they were accommodated. For the others it was often standing room only.

Perhaps a fair indication of the level of talent often available in drama groups across the years lies in the fact that at least three of the players — Marcie Olive, Joni Yeater, and Gale Stahlhugh — went on to act on and off Broadway.

Dramas presented by the Edyvean troupe and Covenant Players over the years included "Construction," "It Should Happen to a Dog," "A Cup of Trembling," "Christ in the Concrete City," "Godspell," "Our Town," The Builders," "J.B.," "Death of a Salesman," "Of Mice and Men," "The Fantasticks," "Glass Menagerie," "Abraham, Martin, and John," "The Town Dump," "Inherit the Wind," and "You're a Good Man, Charlie Brown."

Institute leaders found that the dramatic presentation of biblical truths often had a far more profound effect than did reading Bible stories or listening to sermons.

Drama Has a Compelling Impact

"I remember more in terms of messages from that summer of drama ... than all the sermons from the previous three years that I went to camp.

"I really remembered the dramas, and it was at that point that I really committed myself.... With the theater, I had discovered my niche. I remember telling my high school teacher I had decided to become an English teacher, and I was going to do theater, and I would also find a way to do religious drama.

"I majored in speech and theater all through Ball State University."

Gail Sturm

Note: Gale went on to teach theater and speech at Lawrence Central High School in Indianapolis.

"Although I had enrolled in seminary, I was unsure about entering the ministry. However, the spiritual impact that came from participating in the drama troupe during two summers at Epworth Forest convinced me that the ordained ministry was, indeed, where I belonged."

David St. John

"Before I came to Epworth Forest that first year I did theater for the whole school year every year and really enjoyed a summer recess from drama. But after that first week of doing drama at Epworth, I decided I'd rather do that than anything else. I was inspired to go up there every year."

Dick Burck

Note: Burck was Dr. Edyvean's technical director at Institute for twenty years.

Burck also tells of the impact of Institute dramas on his son, Doug:

"Doug, went to Epworth three or four years to help with the drama troupe. He was not reverent — far from it. In fact, his irreverence got him into trouble there more than once. However, the only spiritual experience Doug remembers from his youth happened at Epworth! It's simply a place where things like that happen, things that happen nowhere else."

As a final word about what God has done through Institute, perhaps these words by the late Traci Pattison best portray just how real and personal and empowering Christ can become.

The daughter of Deloris (Dee) and John Pattison, Traci loved Epworth Forest more than any other place on earth. Like many pastor's children, she found it a place of security through her family's moves from one pastorate to another and a refuge through the storms of adolescence.

It was at Epworth Forest on August 7, 1970 that Traci made a personal commitment to serve God by doing social work with the underprivileged. She wrote herself the following letter the night she made that commitment:

"Trace,

"Ya' know? You're going to need a friend, a really good and true friend. You know as well as I, that in this grousome (sic) nation, city, and world, you're going to need something, someone, bigger and better than any human being. It's got to be God, Trace, and only He can help in the mess we're in!

"Ya' know" its going to be rough. Any Christian has to lead a rough life. But, Trace, with God on your side, you can't lose, you just can't."

"You say you feel as though you've been called to work as a social worker, with the inner city. Well, O.K., DO IT! But, don't let down the guy that gave you the idea! Meaning Jesus Christ!

"You can do it Trace, but, only with God.
A Friend Always,

Traci"

> Note: Traci was tragically killed in a car-train accident just forty-eight days after writing that letter. But her Christ-filled spirit, much of it nurtured and developed at Epworth Forest, lives on in a slim little volume she left behind called *Teen Trace*.

The Forest is definitely aflame in Institute.

Chapter 3

Epworth Forest In Africa Nyembo Christian Conference Center Congo

A new Forest Aflame is currently under construction in Africa in the Congo. Nyembo Christian Conference Center, the dream of missionaries Rev. John and Kendra Enright, is rapidly taking shape and should be completed very soon, if the volatile political situation there permits.

John Enright's connection with Epworth Forest began at age ten. The year was 1960. His missionary parents, Kenneth and Irene Enright, spent six weeks at Epworth Forest during the summer of that year. Ken was the "Missionary on Grounds," teaching two mission classes each day and acquainting Instituters with life in Africa.

Ken Enright was a most powerful and inspiring preacher. On Missionary Night, Wednesday of each week, he challenged Instituters to make a total commitment of life to Jesus Christ and to follow Him wherever He would lead them. On one Wednesday night alone Ken kindled such enthusiasm that over a hundred youth responded to God's call to become missionaries. "He is," as son John remarks, "a legend in his own time."

John remembers his first time at Epworth Forest well. He was his father's African dancer every Wednesday night. Dressed in authentic costume, he danced Lunda dances. In Africa he lived every day with the Lunda people, so he knew the dances well. His legs flew, his arms gyrated, and his feet stomped to the beat of the drum. He was unforgettable.

Five years later, in 1965, the Enrights were back at Epworth Forest. Ken was again the "Missionary on Grounds." John expected to be a dancer again. Only now he was a teenager. He didn't feel quite the same about dancing as he had at age ten.

As things turned out, that summer became what John later called "God's summer" for him. And it all started with a simple invitation. The pastor of Fort Wayne Simpson Church came to call on the Enrights one day. "John," he said, "why don't you come and live with our Simpson youth? We'd be glad to have you." It was an invitation the pastor didn't have to make twice.

So John suddenly found himself a true Instituter — an insider rather than an outsider. The togetherness of being with new friends at Morning Watch, breakfast, classes, sports events, assembly — all of it was wonderful!

But perhaps even more wonderful than that togetherness was the deep spiritual impact the week had on John. He still remembers the theme for the week. It was "The Kingdom of God."

Having grown up in poverty-stricken Zaire, (now Congo), at age 15 he was reacting negatively to an America that seemed focused only on material wealth and success. The Kingdom of God theme and the call to sacrificial, Christlike living were things John could embrace whole-heartedly. And did.

Commitment Night that year was a true highlight for John. Although he will still not reveal what he wrote in his Commitment Night letter to himself, the memory of that letter remains vivid and real to this day.

John grew up, attended college and seminary, pastored churches, and eventually returned to Zaire as a missionary with his wife, Kendra. Life was hard but good. The Enrights were happy missionaries.

Years passed. John and Kendra had become seasoned missionaries with a young family when, a few years ago, a turning point arrived, a crisis.

True, it might not have seemed like a crisis to most people. The United Methodist Church in Zaire was experiencing phenomenal growth, the kind of growth parent churches in the USA only dream about. Seventy congregations had multiplied to over 1,600! A few thousand members had exploded to over 700,000! Incredible!

However, the burgeoning numbers concealed some deeply disturbing problems. John was gravely concerned that too many Zairian Christians were more nominal than faithful. He struggled with how to help bring Christian leaders there to a higher commitment to the person and ways of Jesus. Here is his story, as related in an interview done in 1997:

"In Zaire the traditional (materialistic) world view is adopted by most Christians. That became sadly obvious one day when I was teaching a class of thirty-three Zairian pastors at the Kafakumba training school.

" 'How many of you,' I asked, 'at this very instant would be willing to leave for the USA and never come back; never see your families again?' I expected two or three might raise their hands. How wrong I was! All thirty-three hands shot up!

"So I began to wonder: How can we help the Christians in Zaire to learn and live the true story of Jesus? It is a difficult question because they are very aware of how people live in the USA and they want to be like them in many ways that are not Christian. The appeal of prosperity is so great in the midst of poverty.

"That's when Epworth Forest flashed through my brain. I thought, We need Epworth Forest in Zaire! A place like Epworth Forest can help us teach and live the true story of Jesus, whose primary ministry was to 'the least of these.'

"That was several years ago. We've been working at that dream for more than ten years now and it is over 60% complete. Our Epworth Forest in Africa will be independent and self supporting.

"Our hydroelectric plant is up and running! It gives 24-hour electricity, a major miracle in Zaire. The auditorium will seat 1000 people. Equipment for the cafeteria and dining hall has already been purchased. Eventually there will be cottages to house 500 residents for each event we sponsor.

"Our cornerstone program will be a week-long experience for young people just as at Epworth Forest Institute.

"At another time we will train Sunday School teachers, 500 each time. We have a tremendous need for trained Sunday School teachers. Though we have 1,600 Methodist churches in Zaire, few of them have Sunday Schools!"

"Another time there will be a training school for evangelists. We have already held a convention of medical workers at Nyembo.

23

"To reach the 'least of these' that are far back in the villages we will bring trainees to our center, but only for short periods of time. Limiting training to one week per year means the trainees will not be absent from their villages so long that they refuse to return home. We must never sever the roots our people have in their villages.

"On the other hand, since a one-week training period is so short, we plan to reinforce the training by bringing the same group back to Nyembo year after year. That will enable them to know each other and to become a team.

"Chapter 25 of Matthew's gospel is the key. At the judgment we will be asked how we have benefited the least of these — the hungry, thirsty, stranger, naked, sick, and prisoners. If our doctrine and our work are true to Christ, we will have benefited such folk. Our Nyembo Center will be totally dedicated to serving the "least of these."

"The story of Jesus must remain our basis, whether we live in Zaire or in America. I pray that Epworth Forest in North Webster, Indiana, will never forsake that focus."

> Note: Readers are well aware that in the years since this interview the politi-cal situation in Zaire/Congo has become intensely volatile. The Enrights have had to evacuate their station more than once, but indigenous workers at Nyembo have been able to proceed with the building there, albeit often against enormous odds.
>
> Donations for the renovation of Freeland House, the hotel at Epworth Forest, are being tithed to help with the construction of the Conference Center at Nyembo.

The Forest is aflame in the Congo.

Chapter 4

Re-Yo-Ad

Re-Yo-Ad stands for <u>Re</u>tarded <u>Yo</u>ung <u>Ad</u>ults, another fine camping opportunity for special persons at Epworth Forest. It began in 1965 as Special Education Camp under the direction of George and Martha McDermott of Alexandria First Methodist Church. Their daughter, Elizabeth, was mentally handicapped, and the McDermotts felt led to establish a summer camping experience for her and others like her. There were sixteen campers that first year.

Mentally handicapped persons who attend Re-Yo-Ad are grouped by age: youth, young adults, adults, and older adults. Various age groupings have been tried over the years, but normally youth are ages 15-20; young adults, 21-30; adults, 30-39; and older adults, 40-60 years old.

The wide spectrum of mental challenges and ages represented by the campers requires complex programming that is extremely sensitivity to campers' needs.

All Re-Yo-Ad activities are planned to teach new skills, increase self-confidence, and provide fun in a supportive, Christian environment. These include crafts, physical fitness, Bible study, music, nature study, hiking, Special Olympics training, drama, and swimming.

However, all who have ever experienced Re-Yo-Ad, either as participants or as adult staff, will tell you that the camp is much, much more.

The Flavor Of Re-Yo-Ad

Though it is impossible to describe adequately the spiritual flavor of this remarkable camp, Martha McDermott tries:

"Love became the keynote of the camp. God had given these young people a great capacity for love, and they shared unreservedly with us and received ours without question."

Evidence that the campers' generous love blessed the staff as well as the campers follows:

"The Christian volunteer counselors were so wonderful! God led us to them, or them to us. Many only had two weeks of vacation and gave one of those weeks to Re-Yo-Ad.

"At the end of camp one year a young counselor declared, 'I have never felt so completely myself in my life. I hate to go back to the real world!'

Mrs. McDermott's account of the healing, Spirit-filled impact of one very special morning worship at Re-Yo-Ad bears further witness to such blessings:

"One very dedicated young man on our staff had recently lost his son in death — his first child. Despite his grief, he had kept his commitment to serve as one of our counselors.

"As I stood on the auditorium stage leading worship one morning, I suddenly had the sense that God was very near. We were singing, 'How Great Thou Art' at the time.

"I happened to look down at this young man singing so bravely with tears streaming down his face, and suddenly it seemed that he was enveloped in a great light!

"When worship was over, I walked to breakfast with another staff person and shared with him what I had seen. He replied, 'Oh, Martha, I saw that light! It was all around you, too!'" Surely the Spirit of the Lord was at Re-Yo-Ad that day.

Martha McDermott concludes: "George and I both grew in faith and joy in this work. The song, 'Only Believe' became George's testimony of faith." According to those who knew them best, it was a testimony the McDermotts gave every day of their long years of service to Re-Yo-Ad.

The camp and its staff have changed over the years, but its impact has continued to be a very special one, as borne out by the two stories that follow:

Twenty Plus Precious Years

"One of the greatest parts of my life has come from my opportunity to counsel at Camp Re-Yo-Ad more than twenty years in the Young Adult Section.

"The tremendous, loving staff comes from wherever! The McDermotts, who founded the camp, were absolutely super and were so gifted and giving. Rev. Ross Richey, my good friend who is now deceased, was with us in the very first camp. Others included Rex Bowman, a Baptist layman from Lafayette, Joyle Allen, a retired school teacher from Markle UMC, 'Father' Dave Fletcher, our Roman Catholic director from Florida, and Rev. John Wagner, who then served at Epworth UMC in South Bend.

"Year after year Epworth Forest summer staff persons say they enjoy Camp Re-Yo-Ad more than any other event.

"Of course there are many moments of testing, and you always go home dead tired at the end of the week, but those are nothing compared with the feeling of inward peace and love you also take home.

"Knowing you have helped bait a hook for a fishing class, helped write a letter home, listened to the same stories over and over, and seen eyes light up when picture taking time rolls around — these are never-to-be-forgotten rewards.

"And sing! Do they ever love to sing! That bunch of Re-Yo-Ad campers is by far my best, most responsive congregation of the whole year, year after year! And you never have trouble getting volunteers to raise the flag in the morning or give grace for a meal.

"What's more, Re-Yo-Ad is the most interfaith, interracial, and inter-generational camping you can imagine.

"Epworth Forest has truly become home away from home for many of our campers. For a whole year they look forward joyfully to the next year's event. I get more hugs in one week at Re-Yo-Ad than I get the other fifty-one weeks put together. When camp is over I get a veritable flood of phone calls, cards, and letters of thanksgiving. It is truly humbling to receive that much love.

"Countless lives have been touched by God's love as Re-Yo-Ad campers, counselors, and directors all blend their lives together in loving, laughing, crying, working, and playing together.

"Sometimes I hear the phrase 'Special People' spoken with derogatory intent. Those of us who have been touched by Camp Re-Yo-Ad have learned by loving experience just how special these 'Special People' really are!"

"May Re-Yo-Ad continue for many generations to come: that is my prayer."

Ron Bowman

A Memorable Performance

"I will never forget the day I interrupted a particularly hectic schedule to accept an invitation to a talent show presented by the campers at Re-Yo-Ad.

"We weren't very far into the program before I a found myself getting more than a little distracted. My eyes kept straying to a somewhat overweight woman of about forty sitting among the prospective performers. This woman's full attention was riveted on something in her lap — a small doll. Rocking back and forth, back and forth, this woman lovingly cradled the doll much as any four-year-old child would. Through act after act she sat there, cradling and rocking, rocking and cradling.

"When her turn to perform finally came, she stood up, carefully deposited the doll in her chair, and stepped to the microphone.

"What followed nearly blew me away. It was the most professional, the most moving rendition of 'You'll Never Walk Alone' I had ever heard!

"When the woman finished, she returned to her chair, carefully picked up the doll, sat down, and began again cradling and rocking it, apparently quite unaware of the applause or of how utterly stunning her performance had been.

"In that moment I gained a much keener awareness of how God's precious and wonderful gifts are sometimes hidden in the most unpretentious and unlikely people. It was humbling and gratifying all at the same time. I never cease to be amazed at how Christian love and understanding in our Epworth Forest camps releases God's gifts as blessings to everyone."

Bob Glass

The Forest is aflame with Re-Yo-Ad.

Chapter 5

Royal Family Kids Camp

Royal Family Kids Camp is a one-week residential camp for abused and neglected children from all over northern Indiana. All campers come from foster homes. All have enormous needs. All are recommended by social service agencies.

It was Russ Reahard who first brought Royal Family Kids Camps to the attention of the North Indiana Conference. Russ learned about RFKCs while attending a Christian Camping International Conference late in the 1980s. There were eight such camps scattered around the country at that time. Russ felt that Epworth Forest would be an ideal place for another.

Rev. Robin Smith and Rev. Mike Cover were instrumental in starting the program at Epworth Forest in June of 1991. Rev. Mike Malone has also been a key leader.

Twenty-five youth attended the first year. The enrollment has ranged somewhere between twenty and thirty each year since.

RFKC has Advance Special status. The campers pay nothing.

The children who are admitted to RFKC are often deeply scarred emotionally and otherwise. They require a lot of supervision, a lot of discipline, a lot of understanding, and a lot of love. And, to quote I Corinthians 13, "the greatest of these is love." Vickie Scearce, one of the camp coordinators, put it like this: "Our main purpose . . . is to show God's love through our actions and (to show) that there are adults in the world who can be trusted."

The ratio of counselors to youth is necessarily quite high: one counselor for every two campers. If directors and other staff are counted into that ratio, it is more like 1.5 to 1. New volunteers are often needed in order to maintain that ratio.

Not only do all campers have personal counselors. They also have a special "Grandma" and "Grandpa" for the entire time they are at camp.

The week's schedule includes Bible classes, activity centers, swimming, fishing, group games, and horseback riding. There is also a ride around Lake Webster on the paddle wheel boat "Dixie."

Near the end of the week the staff gives a big birthday bash for all campers, who later return to their foster homes with gifts and memories of a week unlike any others in their often difficult lives.

Three stories make this camp come alive.

A Precious Parting Gift

"Many of the children who attend Royal Family Kids Camp are caught up in patterns of acting out behavior that continue during the camp.

"I remember in particular one boy who attended camp for several years and often challenged the staff with his rebellious behavior. When this boy turned 12 and came to camp for his last eligible year, he secreted a large, highly prized squirt gun in his luggage, even though he knew that squirt guns were not permitted. Ultimately the gun was discovered and placed in safe keeping until such time as the boy would return to his foster home.

"At the end of the week we held a closing ceremony which recognized those who had reached age 12 and would not be coming back the following year.

"At that ceremony this particular boy tearfully announced that he wanted to give his treasured squirt gun to the camp! The fact that squirt guns were forbidden at camp was quite beside the point. To the staff the spirit of gratitude reflected in that boy was a clear indication of the transforming power of God's grace."

A Softened Heart

"The camp is unapologetically a Christian camp.

"One counselor had a girl who, at the beginning of camp, announced flatly that she did not want to be a Christian. She had experienced bad treatment at the hands of rigid and judgmental Christians and did not want to be like them, she said.

"(However,) by the end of a week of experiencing floods of God's unconditional, self-giving love from an often tired and tried staff, the girl had changed her mind. She said she was ready to let Jesus into her heart, ready to become a Christian."

The Power of Example

"One middle-aged couple who had recently been engaged came as counselors one year. They were obviously very much in love. But both expressed concern that their loving relationship might get in the way of the campers' experiences and even entertained the idea that they would not share the fact that they were engaged.

"However, word leaked out, and God used their relationship in a wonderful way.

"Several young girls were able to see what a Christian male-female relationship was like. The women counselors were able to talk with them in a way that would not have been possible without the example of the engaged couple."

Mike Malone, supplied all three stories.

In summarizing the impact of RFKC, Camp Coordinator, Vickie Scearce, once said, "We don't know what good comes from the week, but hopefully we have given these children something to hang onto, so God can cause it to flourish."

Apparently that is often the case. Foster parents frequently report that the children come home with a more positive attitude, that their self-esteem is noticeably improved, and that they are often better able to handle some of their problems.

Maybe that's because they have learned that they really are God's kids — members of His Royal Family.

The Forest is aflame in Royal Family Kids Camp.

Chapter 6

Choir School

Epworth Forest Choir School is not well named, for it is much more than a choir school. It is more than a place where people learn to become better choir members or better choir directors. The exact nature of the "much more" is, however, difficult to articulate.

Only those who have been to Choir School can fully understand this. Even veterans of ten or fifteen years, for whom it has become an integral part of Christian life, often cannot find the right words. It's that good, that amazing, that surprising, and that transforming!

It is important to begin with Varner Chance, the founder of Choir School.

Of course, Varner would immediately add the name of his wife, Anna, who has carried a full share of the combined ministry. And he would also include the name of his daughter, Rebecca (Carrington) who, like her mother, served Choir School faithfully in a number of capacities for many years. Likewise he would graciously acknowledge the countless people who served in leadership roles of many kinds — the personnel infrastructure of Choir School, you might call it.

But again, it is important to begin with Varner Chance, the founder of Choir School. Seldom can "founder" be applied so appropriately!

Varner's music ministry at Epworth Forest began not in Choir School but at Senior High Institute. From 1940 through 1966 he devoted six strenuous weeks of each summer to directing and nurturing Institute choirs. Singing in his choir often became the single most passionate desire of Instituters.

Meanwhile the dream of having a Choir School at Epworth Forest became ever more compelling to Varner. A place where choir directors of small churches could be introduced to great

33

Christian repertoire, a place where a mass choir could sing that repertoire, a place for training church musicians who might never have a similar opportunity anywhere else — that was his dream.

And it was a unique one at the time. It took some persuading to sell the dream. But in 1952 such a school was officially recommended. For three years thereafter Varner and George Fenstermacher, Executive Director of Epworth Forest Foundation, worked on the master plan for the school. In the summer of 1955, the Epworth Forest Choir School made its debut.

That first year enrollment totaled seventy-five. It jumped to ninety-six the following year. And within a few more years it reached 250!

In addition to participants from many parts of Indiana, Choir School has drawn people from twenty other states and from foreign countries as well. The Netherlands has sent the most, but Germany, France, Austria, England, Canada, and Korea have all had their participants.

Not only do Choir School concerts thrill audiences at Epworth Forest. Sounds of Hope, its touring group, inspired and blessed audiences in many European cities for years.

A variety of groups and leaders emerged as Choir School developed through the years. In addition to Mixed Choir, Women's Choir, Children's Laboratory Choir, String Orchestra, Hand bell Choir, sectional leaders, Counselor/Devotional Leader, Chaplain, Organist, and an Assistant Director — all of these, and more, were part of Choir School at one time or another.

And the spectrum of classes offered was wide. In 1979, for example, there were classes in conducting, voice, organ literature, choral reading, Christian symbolism in worship, selection of music, bell choir, and auditorium and staging.

"Members were expected to be prepared to grow musically, spiritually, and socially," according to the 25th Anniversary Concert brochure. The fact that many have come back year after year to be enriched by the challenges they find at Choir School bears evidence to that growth.

Choir School has focused on the performance of excellent Christian music throughout its history. Participants go home armed with packets bulging with quality selections that can be used in a variety of churches and choirs.

But there is also a lighter side to Choir School for those who wish to participate in it: "Showboat" has been a delightful Saturday evening extravaganza and a rich tradition through the years. This musical revue customarily features light music, dancing, skits, and general good fun.

For years "Showboat" was performed from the upper deck of the paddle wheeler "Dixie." Enthusiastic audiences lined the shore at North Webster. More recently, it has been performed in the great amphitheater at Epworth Forest.

Varner Chance's fortieth year with Choir School, and his last, was 1994. Choir School has been most fortunate in finding capable people to follow Varner since his retirement. Chuck (Charles) Scott served as Administrative Director from 1995 through 1998. Kim LaRue took over that position in 1999.

It is impossible to quantify the impact of Choir School. But perhaps a few stories will help:

A Choir School in the Pacific Northwest

"I met the Chances in the mid-60's. I had just finished my M. Mus. degree at Indiana University and hired on at Illinois State U. in Normal. Varner was directing the choir of Wesley UMC in nearby Bloomington. Soon Choir School (at Epworth Forest) was on the agenda for two or three summers; then a Sounds of Hope tour in 1972.

"The notion that the Choir School model could be adopted in the Pacific Northwest Annual Conference was put to the test in 1979. With two other co-founders, we launched Jubilate — a festival and retreat of worship and the arts. Jubilate has met every summer since, sometimes in Spokane, sometimes in Tacoma.

"... It has been enormously satisfying to be a part of all this (and) ... a delight to reflect on the place Chances and Choir School have in my life!"

Dr. Tom Richardson, Moscow, ID

Three Girls Make a Difficult Decision

"One year three girls who came to Choir School got into trouble by sneaking out of camp one night to be with their boyfriends. The boys were not a part of Choir School; they had simply driven up to be with these girls. And they had brought their drugs with them.

"Someone patrolling the grounds caught the girls and brought them to me for disciplining.

"In talking with the girls, it became obvious that their relationships with these boys were pretty serious. But I became more and more disturbed by the kind of people the boys seemed to be. It was obvious that theirs was not a good influence. I expressed my concern to the girls, and in the end I presented these three options:

1. The girls could leave Choir School and go back home with their boyfriends.

2. They could send their boyfriends home.

3. They could remain in Choir School but promise not to see their boyfriends any more.

"The girls went back to their cottage to think things over.

"By the next morning all three had made the decision to remain at Choir School and not see the boys again. All three stuck by that decision.

"The fact that this was a very important choice to make at that point in their lives was borne out later when I received a plaque from one of the girls which read, 'If God is your Father, Christ is your Brother.' On the back was a personal message: 'To a man who has helped me to grow! I love ya and I'll never forget ya! Love always, _____.'

"We have a lot of memorabilia that we have accumulated through the years, but none is more precious than that plaque."

Varner Chance

A Mutual Blessing

Both Varner and Anna testify eagerly to the impact Choir School has had on their lives.

"We have received very deep meaning in our lives, each year richer and deeper than the previous one. A big part of this impact on us came from what we saw happening constantly in others from God. It gave us hope for the future.

"Choir School feeds the roots of many wonderful Christians, and they, by enriching the singing of their churches, feed the roots of many more Christians."

And as for the way others feel about the Chances ...

These words of thanks written to them as Choir School entered its 30th year weave a fitting close to this chapter of Epworth Forest history:

> *A rose touched by the sun's warm rays,*
> *all its petals gently doth unfold.*
> *So you when touched by God's great mercy,*
> *let joy and gladness fill your souls.*
> *For the thirty years of joy and gladness in song we call*
> *CHOIR SCHOOL — we thank you!*
>
> Kathryn DeLawter

The Forest is aflame at Choir School.

Chapter 7

Camp Adventure

Camp Adventure for junior high/middle school youth has roots in Boyville and Girlville, once held on the grounds of Epworth Forest. These long-standing camps merged into coeducational Camp Adventure in 1941.

The story of Camp Adventure's beginnings need not be repeated here. It is carefully described both in W. B. Freeland's *Epworth Forest, The First Twenty-five Years* and in Manifold's book, *Epworth Forest, The First Fifty Years*.

During the period covered by this current book, 1968-99, Camp Adventure has been located at Epworth Heights on Backwater Lake about five miles southeast of Epworth Forest.

Camp Adventure lives in the rich shadow of Senior High Institute, our largest camping program. Yet junior high camping for many years has been second only to Institute in numbers of youth participants.

Camp Adventure is, by design, a more primitive type of camping than Senior High Institute. The camp makes far more use of the outdoors, particularly in its Home-in-the-Woods program, which is carefully described in Manifold's history mentioned above.

Recent Improvements
At Camp Adventure

In 1989 a kitchen fire destroyed Lookout Lodge, the gathering place, kitchen, and eating location for the camp. For a year after this disaster, the camp was forced to use a pole barn and have food catered in.

Even before the fire in Lookout Lodge, plans were underway to improve or replace the Manager's house. So both building projects were handled together.

The all-new Manager's house was completed in 1991, and the new Lookout Lodge was ready for use in 1992. Improvements to the Lodge include winterizing the building and adding sleeping quarters for forty. Until then, Camp Adventure could schedule no winter activities. Both new structures are much-needed improvements over their predecessors.

Stories From Camp Adventure

In keeping with the theme of this current history, we would like to relate some stories of lives that have been positively impacted at Camp Adventure, both at its present location and at Epworth Forest.

"I remember attending an early Camp Adventure at Epworth Heights. Boy, it was wonderful! I really enjoyed myself and, more important, I found God. It was really neat. I met some wonderful people there and we all went camping way out in that swamp! I guess they still do that."

Gale Sturm

Yes, Gale, they still do. Though the swamp isn't really such a swamp anymore.

A Counselor is Renewed

"You know that so much of what happens at Camp Adventure happens in our 'Home in the Woods' groups. Many Camp Adventure leaders — but not all — conduct a service of invitation to commitment to Christ at the close of the week similar to what we do at Institute.

"I was returning with my group to our 'Home in the Woods' after the commitment service one year. It was a high moment because many young people had responded.

"A counselor stopped me as I was walking with my group and said she wanted to speak to me later that evening.

"When we met she said, 'I'm glad for the experience of counseling this year. It's not only for the opportunity of sharing with

40

the kids but for its impact on my own personal relationship with Christ.'

"She continued: 'Christ came into my life in such a wonderful way when I was in junior high. I was encouraged to share that experience with anyone important to me. So I told my family about it, but I especially wanted to tell my pastor.'

" 'When I had the chance I went to him and told how my life had changed and how real Jesus had become to me. My pastor listened without interruption. But when I was finished, he simply said, "You'll get over it some day." '

" 'I was devastated!'

" 'This Camp Adventure is for kids, but it is also for me. It has renewed my faith in Jesus Christ. I know He is really real and will walk with me and with these kids always. Tonight I could pray and think and tell the kids that they can trust Jesus. It was wonderful!' "

Clyde Trumbauer

A "Tough Guy" and a Deck of Cards

"One of the boys who came to Camp Adventure one year was a real 'tough guy.' On the first night in camp that week, Sunday night, the boy, wanting to show off, gathered some kids around a table and pulled out a deck of cards he'd brought.

"The pastor with the group told him quite simply, 'We don't play cards here.'

"The boy was really upset. He jammed the cards into his pocket and sulked for the rest of the evening.

"As the week progressed, the pastor watched the boy. He could tell that some of the camp activities were strange for him. But increasingly, the boy seemed to be trying to fit in. His tough veneer faded.

"On the last night, Commitment Night, when it came time to share, the boy amazed everybody by saying that he really liked what he had seen at camp that week. But it was what he said next that truly shocked them: 'I know that God has come into my life this week,' he said. 'I'm glad that I came.'

"Then he pulled out his deck of cards and declared he didn't want to play cards any more. He wanted to burn the whole deck as part of his dedication to God.

"So the cottagers burned those cards in the center of the room that night. But before the deck was completely consumed, the pastor pulled out one half-burned card.

"Several years later he showed it to me when telling this story. He had carried it with him for years as a reminder of that boy's changed life!"

Chuck Hefley

Calls to Ministry

"For me Camp Adventure was truly a transforming place. In 1992 I was invited to be a counselor there for a week. I wasn't yet a United Methodist. But I was a good friend of the camp director's sister. Maybe that's why I was invited.

"I was twenty and had a good job with an advertising agency. I thought I was happy and satisfied in my work.

"But a week away at a kid's camp sounded like it might be interesting. So I accepted the invitation and took a week off from work. I hadn't the slightest hint of what that week would bring.

"That year there was a custom at Camp Adventure — at least, there was during the week I was there. It happened around the campfire. Youth and adults alike were asked to focus on receiving and giving forgiveness. We were encouraged to write down one particularly troublesome problem on a piece of paper. The minutes of silence given for the task were holy. Each person's writing was confidential.

"Then we all burned our papers in the campfire as a sign of God's forgiveness. Afterward anyone who wished could share the problem they had written about. The Holy Spirit was present with great power.

"I could not stop thinking about my secular job that night. I realized that it was distracting me as a counselor. In fact, it was distracting my whole life. I felt unhappy and unfulfilled.

"I asked my fellow counselors and the camp director to pray for me. And after that prayer session I felt a clear call from God. I was certain in my heart that my future was to be in ministry to young people.

T. Scott Greene
current Director/Manager of Camp Adventure

Many youth made life-changing commitments to Jesus Christ at Camp Adventure before making similar commitments at Institute. Loretta Gruver, recently retired lifelong nursing missionary to Liberia, was one of them. Michael Coyner, current Bishop of the Dakota Area, was another. And there were more . . .

"I retired at the 1984 session of Annual Conference. Rev. Jim Evans was ordained elder at the same conference session. Jim came up to me at the reception party for those just ordained.

"I said to him, 'The Lord bless you in your ministry, Jim.' (That's the way Brother Clyde really talks!)

"Jim said, 'It's good to see you, Brother Clyde. For a long time I've been meaning to talk to you.'

"Jim went on, 'The last year Camp Adventure was at Epworth Forest you were the preacher and camp director. That was when I received Christ into my life, and it was also when I was called into the ministry. I just wanted you to know what an influence you had on me.'

"'I praise the Lord for that one,' said Brother Clyde. 'It's fun to be the instrument, but you know you're not the real power. Christ is.' "

Clyde Trumbauer

The Forest is aflame at Camp Adventure.

Chapter 8

Camp Inclusion

Camp Inclusion was held at Epworth Forest in 1977, 1978, and 1979. It was what the people of Trinity United Methodist Church in Muncie, Indiana, called their "creative offering" to the North Indiana Conference. Trinity was one of five predominantly African-American congregations in the Conference at the time.

The nation was in heightened racial turmoil during the 1960s, 1970s and 1980s. That turmoil was felt with greater or lesser intensity all over Indiana.

Rev. J. C. Williams, then pastor of Trinity U. M. C., says: "The American scene during the 60s, 70s, and 80s ... was fearful, hectic and stubbornly in need of general and institutional change as related to the diversity of ethnic, racial and cultural grouping.

"African-Americans ... were not being heard or adequately respected as a people. This was reflected whenever or wherever we were involved with Caucasians in mutual endeavors.

"Thus, Camp Inclusion was one of our creative responses to the times — a response wherein we insisted on equal relationships and communication based on our Christian commitments."

The roster of resource people for this interracial, intergenerational camp was impressive. It included J. C. Williams, Jacob C. Williams, Jr., Charles McPeek, Vivian Conley, Leon Hartman, Dennis Ingle, Merrell Geible, Gessel Berry, Maceo Pembroke, Ron VerLee, James W. Williams, Virgil Bjork, Edna Bradley, Fred Dare, Tom Weigand, James Swingley, Riley Case, Anita Fenstermacher, Luther Bradley, Sr., Pat Kyle, Robert Davis, Gary Forbes, Roosevelt Jackson, Wayne Stevens, John Taylor, James Taylor, Glen Ingle, Saundra White, Gerald Jones, Roderick McLean, Alice Conley, and Rosamae Williams.

The Camp Inclusion Study Book was prepared by J. C. Williams and his wife, Rosamae. It was based on the "Seven Greatest Sins" teachings of the revered Indian mystic and champion of non-violence, Mohandas K. Gandhi. Words and works of Martin Luther King, Jr. also figured heavily in the curriculum.

Campers were introduced to many African-American customs, mores, and traditions, among them the not-yet-popular Kwanzaa celebration.

> Note: It is interesting to realize that African-American leaders in North Indiana were teaching the seven principles of Kwanzaa as a Christian alternative to the pervasive commercialism of Christmas over 20 years ago.

Menus for the week had a definite "soul" flavor: Carolina hash browns, Deep South pork neck bones, Kentucky sausage, south Georgia grits, Southern corn bread, chicken, flap jacks, and Tennessee hot biscuits were some of the foods served.

Many high moments marked the three-year duration of Camp Inclusion. Two occurred on the final nights of the camp in 1979.

The first featured a mass choir celebration using African-American worship styles and music. All churches in the North Indiana Conference were invited to send singers to that moving celebration. The second featured "World Without End," an elaborately costumed ethnic drama based on the life of Jesus Christ and written by James Wesley Williams, (a son of J. C. and Rosamae Williams).

Clearly, Camp Inclusion provided a bold and deep immersion into black culture. The impact of that immersion, at least for one camper, is seen in the following story:

An Incredible Eye-Opening Experience

"I was very young, about twelve or thirteen, and very naive ... I grew up in a very, very small town. There was not one black person in town, so there was never a racial issue because we were never confronted, never exposed.

"So this Camp Inclusion came along and my mom (Anita Fenstermacher) tried to bridge the cultural gaps and get me exposed to diversity.

"I was very excited. I wanted to participate, but I was scared to death. I didn't stay for the whole week. It was so foreign to me!

"I fell in love with J. C. Williams. I found him so spiritual. I saw in him qualities that I never had seen or ever been exposed to in my own church, and not even at Institutes.

"I was so incredibly curious. I was almost consumed with the need to learn, to observe....

"That experience had a huge impact on my life. I viewed a different culture, a different way of spirituality.

"The singing was incredible! There was something there! I needed whatever it was in my own church, but because of segregation we never had (it).

"This was an opportunity. This was a time at Epworth where I was able to walk on the soil of Epworth Forest and see diversity for the first time and feel very safe in that environment. It was just an incredible experience!"

Liz Gatarana

Founder J. C. Williams assesses the impact of Camp Inclusion in these words: "Many of the youth who were campers (there). . . are now ministers, educators, attorneys, social and criminal justice professionals, and strong members of the laity in various local churches."

He goes on: "I firmly affirm (that) Camp Inclusion was one of the creative instruments for social change ... in the North Indiana Conference...."

That's no small accomplishment for any camp, any where, anytime.

The Forest was aflame in Camp Inclusion.

Chapter 9

Deaf Camps

The first Epworth Forest Deaf Camp took place on Labor Day weekend, 1973. The original stimulus for that camp came from an incident that occurred in the parsonage of Goshen First U. M. C. one spring afternoon six years earlier. That was the afternoon pastor's wife Grace Nunery suddenly found herself face-to-face with a couple who would not talk to her ... because they couldn't hear her.

It was a Sunday in Lent. Husband Al had left to take their son Bill back to college. Grace was busy preparing her part in the upcoming evening service when she heard a knock at the door. Opening it, she found two strangers, a man and a woman, standing on her porch. One of them handed her a note. It read, "May we see Reverend Nunery?"

Grace invited the couple in and began to explain that her husband was away. Very quickly it became obvious that neither of her guests understood a single word she was saying. Grabbing paper and pen, Grace launched into what would turn out to be a very long afternoon of exchanging notes with the gracious but silent couple.

The first notes they exchanged explained why the couple had come: Al Nunery had conducted the funeral of the woman's father. The woman had appreciated the service and wanted to see Al again. (Grace remembered that funeral, although it had happened fully a year earlier. Done at the request of a local funeral director for a non-member of the church, it had given Al his first experience in working with an interpreter — a signer.)

After that initial exchange of information, Grace and her pleasant guests pursued many topics through "note talk." When those finally ran out, she racked her brain for more ways to entertain them. So she took them on a tour of the parsonage, showed them her prize African violets, and eventually ended up serving them tea and cake. Through it all she felt frustrated and inadequate because communication with the couple was so difficult.

The time for evening services arrived. Al was still not home, so Grace invited the couple to church. They accepted.

And right then and there was born Grace Nunery's long, love-filled ministry to the hearing impaired, though she was not aware of it at the time.

Things actually went pretty well that Sunday evening in the spring of 1968. In spite of being unable to talk to one another, church members and the deaf couple communicated through notes, smiles, and handshakes. At the end of the evening, Grace invited the couple to come back the following Sunday, although she later confessed she didn't really think there was a chance they would.

But they did! They brought two friends, and they stayed for Grace's Sunday school class!

Even more deaf people came to church and Sunday school the following week. One day during that week some of them showed up at the parsonage with a church bulletin and a list of questions. "What does doxology mean? What is a benediction? What is resurrection?" they wanted to know. Grace did not know where to begin, more feelings of frustration and inadequacy.

During the weeks and months that followed, she struggled to make things easier for her deaf friends to understand. Although the congregation had welcomed them warmly, they were still isolated because they understood so little of what was going on. Sitting in the church balcony and flanked by these seekers, Grace wrote down every word her husband spoke from the pulpit. Too often, however, her notes were received with questioning eyes and puzzled shakes of the head.

In preparing for Sunday school, Grace consulted commentaries, concordances, Bible dictionaries — anything that might elucidate the text of the week. Every Sunday she went to class armed with lots and lots of notes written on lots and lots of newsprint. Again, there were the questioning eyes and puzzled shakes of the head.

One week she was overjoyed to find a tract on the Sermon on the Mount. The topic was right for the upcoming Sunday. The source (American Bible Society) was reliable. The tract seemed especially clear content-wise. So she happily ran off copies, only to find that the print was much too small for her readers. Far worse, though, the content, like Al's sermons, was obviously far from clear to these wonderful, searching souls, more frustration and feelings of inadequacy.

Ultimately there was only one conclusion to make: the Nunerys needed an interpreter, a signer for their deaf friends.

Finding one who could sign abstract spiritual concepts proved difficult, indeed. In addition, those who did finger spelling (signing each letter of a word separately) proved too slow. And those who dutifully interpreted word by word, sentence by sentence, missed the boat too. "You have to cut," the deaf complained on paper. "Too many words!"

The deaf, Grace finally discovered, do not think in sentences complete with articles and conjunctions, adverbs and adjectives. They think in a marvelous mental shorthand that captures the essence of meaning.

The time had come for Grace to learn that shorthand.

"Basically, I learned from the deaf people themselves" she says. But you must realize that I was over fifty at the time. It wasn't easy remembering all those hand and finger positions, all those gestures. I got so frustrated! I made lots of mistakes, some of them funny, some truly embarrassing. But everybody was patient with me, sometimes more patient than I was with myself. We laughed a lot. Sometimes I cried. Finally, we began to communicate, the deaf and I, in the language that was theirs. It was such a relief, such a blessing to us all!"

Five years later, after establishing a ministry to the deaf at Ft. Wayne Forest Park UMC and seeing just how capable and caring deaf people can be in an environment that is loving and supportive, Grace began to wonder why there were no camps for the deaf.

So, determined in this as in everything else, she began her own campaign for a deaf camp. Although she met much resistance, she found a few champions, among them George Fenstermacher. Still the going was tough. After all, who ever heard of a camp for the deaf? And what would the deaf do if they had one? Wouldn't camp life be dangerous for them? Besides, there were protocols to follow.

At the Conference office it was explained, "You can't just start a camp because you want to. You need to plan a new camp at least three years in advance and be awarded a place in the summer schedule. We're full this summer."

"Well, when is your summer over?" asked Grace. She could not answer any of their questions about proposed program, leadership, or funding. Yet her plea, "Give me a try," was so persuasive that she was finally booked into the Epworth Forest calendar for Labor Day weekend that very year, 1973. All other camps had ended by then.

The first deaf camp was for families. Grace was astounded when over eighty deaf persons attended that first year. Volunteers brought food from their gardens; others came to cook. A staff seemed to materialize from nowhere. Grace was able to raise the $300 it cost. And even though she was the only adult signer on the grounds, the weekend was a tremendous success. There were no more struggles for credibility. The second weekend after Labor Day became the established time for Deaf Family Camp and has remained so to this day.

In 1976 Grace began to wonder why camping for the deaf had to be restricted to a single weekend and why children couldn't have a camp of their own. So she planned a week-long camp for deaf children.

Forty-six children ages eight through eighteen showed up that first year of Deaf Camp for Children. It was a good beginning. Because the socialization of deaf children offers a special challenge, the lower age limit was soon dropped to four years (three and a half if the children were potty trained). The upper limit was also dropped to fourteen.

Other camping experiences for the deaf have developed through the years: primitive island camping for fifteen-through 18-year-olds, camps for married couples, and camping bus trips are three examples. Both Epworth Forest and Camp Adventure have been used to accommodate deaf camps.

The North Indiana Conference deaf camps now enjoy such a good reputation that Gallaudet University (the only U. S. university devoted solely to the deaf) carries advertisements for them in some of its literature. Several other institutions do the same.

It's small wonder, then, that campers come from many places in the United States and even from abroad. During one recent year two 15-year-olds from Tel Aviv attended deaf camp for youth, and two years before that two women came over from Denmark.

And now for some stories about campers:

A Little Girl's First Deaf Camp

One summer a little girl from Ohio showed up at Deaf Camp. This little girl had barely set foot in the camp before she saw something that made her stop dead still. There, not three feet away, stood a girl who was signing.

In a frenzy the first little girl grabbed her counselor by the hand and dragged her over to the other child. With hand signs she asked the counselor: "She deaf?"

The counselor signed, "Yes." The little girl's eyes got very large! Seeing a little boy nearby, she signed: "He deaf?"

"Yes," signed the counselor again. And the girl began jumping up and down.

Fairly flying around the room, she pointed to one child after another: "She deaf?" "He deaf?" she asked over and over again.

Every time the answer came back, "Yes." The little girl's joy was uncontrollable.

Until that moment she had been the only deaf person she knew. For the first time in her life she realized that she was not alone in her deafness. There were many other deaf children in the world, too.

That week the cold, hard isolation of that little girl's life began to melt way. In its place came the wonderful experience of true companionship and a sense of Christian community — precious gifts to be cherished for the rest of her life.

> Note: 90% of deaf children have "hearing" parents. Their isolation, like that of the little girl above, is very common, especially in homes where the parents do not sign.

The Deaf Learn that They Can Pray

There was a beautiful young deaf mute woman who one day came to share some serious personal problems with Grace (Nunery). For long minutes on end she signed her misery.

When the woman finally finished signing, Grace encouraged her to pray about her problems. "Just talk to God and ask for His help," she signed.

"Oh, no!" the woman signed in reply. "You don't understand. You're 'hearing' and you can talk. But me — I can't talk, so God wouldn't understand me. Besides, I couldn't hear Him even if He answered me. And I know He doesn't sign!"

Stunned and remorseful, Grace replied, "Oh, I didn't mean that you actually have to talk to God. God knows your mind, your thoughts, your feelings. God made you. He knows your hair, your face, and your fingers. God knows you completely, and he loves you so much. All you need to do is to think your prayers. He will understand, and someday He will answer you."

Suddenly the woman's face lit up in astonishment and relief. God didn't seem so unreachable after all!

Two Deaf Boys Face the Future

Before coming to camp, two teenage deaf boys were asked to write down what they were going to be when they grew up.

The first one wrote, "When I grow up I'm going to be 'hearing.'"

The second wrote, "When I grow up I'm going to be dead."

Neither boy had ever known a deaf person who had reached adulthood!

Imagine their surprise when they got to camp and learned that many deaf teenagers do, indeed, become adults, and that although they may always remain deaf, they can still live full, productive lives.

Word of the success of the Epworth Forest deaf camps has resulted in widespread requests for more information. From Nevada, Mississippi, California, New York, Pennsylvania and other states they come: "We have a deaf neighbor/relative, but there isn't any place around here for them to go camping." "We never heard of a camp for the deaf. What can we do to start one?" Grace Nunery is always more than ready to share her experience and her expertise.

But we wonder: did she have even the slightest inkling back there in 1968 that the visit of two total strangers would open such wide doors of opportunity for so many? We doubt it.

Yes, Bishop White! God is good ... all the time!

The Forest is aflame in deaf camps.

Chapter 10

School Of Christian Mission
United Methodist Women

Every summer for many, many years the United Methodist Women (U. M. W.) and its predecessor, the Women's Society of Christian Service (W. S. C. S.), have conducted a week-long School of Christian Missions (S. C. M.). For most of the historical period of this book, though not currently, the S. C. M. for the North Indiana Conference was held at Epworth Forest.

The S. C. M. was unique among Epworth Forest events because of its strong focus on world missions. In addition, it was the only event that followed a structure and design used by every other annual conference in the nation. In turn, that structure and design was used by every Jurisdictional School of Missions, the venue for training leaders of Conference S. C. M. That hierarchy still remains.

The uniquely powerful S. C. M. model is actually the creation of the Women's Division of the General Board of Global Ministries. Because of its strong relationship with that body, the U. M. W. has become arguably the largest and strongest women's organization in the world, and its women are among the world's best informed about missions.

Every S. C. M. uses the same three mission studies, each of which is new each year. Books and other resources for the studies are planned years in advance.

Once back home, many participants plan and present at least one of the mission studies in their local U. M. W. This is a primary purpose of S. C. M.

All who participate in S. C. M. are struck by the superior quality of teaching/learning about all aspects of missions. Most classes at the jurisdictional level are taught by Persons in Mission,i.e., missionaries, and other prominent church leaders. Strong teams at each level — jurisdictional, conference, and local — carefully plan, conduct, and evaluate each local school.

Although there are women throughout north Indiana who could attest to the spiritual and intellectual growth that occurs at S. C. M., here are reports from and about three who were privileged to experience that growth at Epworth Forest:

"The grounds of Epworth Forest have provided sanctuary for the many women attending S. C. M. The atmosphere is conducive to study, meditation, and spiritual growth.

"The waters of Lake Webster truly refresh us and are a necessary component to relaxing, meditating and playing.

"Freeland House Hotel and its dining room have provided good food and food for the soul. We have spent many hours of fellowship around the tables.

"I personally praise God for my experience at Epworth Forest as a United Methodist Woman. I have felt God's hand on my life for 'just a closer walk.' "

Pat Weeks,
Conference U. M. W. Past President

"The years at School of Christian Mission were times of great growing. [One year] one new U. M. W. officer had just become a United Methodist. She arrived at her first S. C. M. at Epworth Forest carrying a very different Christian background. She had never known anything but the narrow confines of her church.

"At the S. C. M. she grew dramatically! I saw her just BLOOM, and she turned out to be a wonderful officer. All of us grew that way, I think; we just didn't notice it as much in ourselves.

"The school is so enriching, especially our experiences with missionaries. They open up the world as a far wider place than you ever knew was there before. That's important!

"Those of us who carried responsibilities were the biggest winners. We learned more than anyone else. The preparations required of all leaders are hard work; but as you do the work, you are so richly blessed."

Rosemary Manifold

"My wife, Jane, taught in S. C. M. five or six years and attended without missing for more than thirty years. She, like many others, found the lakefront setting and the outstanding speakers refreshing and inspiring.

"When we first entered the ministry, Jane wasn't at all sure she was in the right profession as a minister's wife. However, her experiences of spiritual deepening and her opportunities to give leadership at Epworth Forest — and perhaps most particularly at S. C. M. — gave her far more self-confidence. Ultimately she came to believe she was in precisely the right calling. Epworth Forest often does that to people, whether they are participants or leaders."

The late Bob Fribley

Humor at School of Christian Missions

"I remember one year at School of Christian Missions when a number of younger women in our cottage brought their children. Those young mothers and their children decided to sleep in an upstairs dorm so their noise would not disturb the older women, who slept in a large downstairs bedroom near the kitchen.

"One morning when most cottagers had already departed for classes, a young mother heard screaming from the older women's room and rushed to investigate. Before she arrived, however, the screaming had turned to hysterical laughter.

"What's happening?" she asked as she ran into the room.

"Nothing really. My roommate screamed because she had put on my glasses instead of her own. She was terrified and cried out, 'I can't see! I can't see!'

"But I find you laughing," said the young mother.

"Oh, that! I just told her I hoped she didn't get our teeth mixed up."

Pastors' and Drive-In Day

For many years provisions were made for pastors and others to attend S. C. M. for just one day. A much larger crowd attended on that day than on any other. Some of the week's premier speakers made presentations. Their Mini-classes focused on one or more of the three mission studies. Those who attended got a taste of nearly everything offered at S. C. M., only in smaller doses.

D. A. R. T. for Mission Weekend

D. A. R. T. stands for Designed to Alert, Recruit, and Train for Mission. It is the weekend counterpart of the week-long S. C. M. and is intended for persons who cannot devote an entire week to mission studies.

D. A. R. T. is guided by the same requirements as S. C. M. and teaches the same mission studies. However, fitting enough class time into a Friday afternoon-through-Sunday noon schedule necessarily leaves less time for other things. The national requirements for D. A. R. T. provide for maximum teaching and learning about missions.

D. A. R. T. has been held a few times at Epworth Forest, though it usually meets elsewhere.

Chi-Mi-Ca

Chi-Mi-Ca stands for Children's Missionary Camp. Designed for four-to-twelve-year-old children of those attending S. C. M., this camp has thrived for several years.

Although in one sense, Chi-Mi-Ca is a child-care program, it is so much more. It is actually a sort of School of Christian Missions for kids.

Teachers of the mission studies for the children use new-every-year mission study materials that relate to the same theme materials their mothers use in the adult classes. Children experience their own worship, study, recreation, crafts, and other creative activities — all related to the mission themes of the year.

Teens

During some of the years that S. C. M. was held at Epworth Forest, provisions were made for mission studies for the teenage youth of those who participated in S. C. M. Teens studied age-level mission materials designed for them on the same themes as those studied by adults.

The Forest was aflame in mission programs.

Chapter 11

Conference Youth Rallies

Conference Youth Rallies at Epworth Forest have been hugely popular for several years. The great crowds of youth who attend these rallies bear witness to their enormous appeal. Often more than two thousand youth pour onto the Epworth Forest grounds, coming from every corner of the Conference.

Many young people attend the rallies because they love the campus at Epworth Forest. Some come because their busy summer schedules have caused them to miss Institute. Some come because the rallies give them one last opportunity to see Christian friends made at Institute before fall and winter activities claim their attention. And some just come.

Customarily these rallies feature worship, workshops, dinner, and lots of Christian fellowship. The most obvious attraction to these September Sunday events, however, is usually a rock concert by a well-known Christian band whose music fills the campground with throbbing beat and decibel levels that threaten to shatter the sound barrier. The kids love it!

Although older Christians may wonder whether such an ambience can possibly provide an authentic Christian experience, it is obvious that each rally has a definite spiritual flavor. Each provides a fervent, exciting atmosphere in which to hear the challenge of loyalty to Christ. Many young people have spiritual experiences at these rallies that reinforce commitments they made at Institute.

Unfortunately we do not have any stories from rally participants, but we do have a story about what happened to a rock band one year. If nothing else, it shows that even popular performers sometimes need help with setting priorities.

A Rainy Day, A Rock Group, And The Jesus Statue

Dave Marty, Epworth Forest Director for several years, recalls one of the several youth rallies that Rev. Jack Scott helped organize and lead — one which gave the featured rock group some real food for thought.

"One rally day the weather was pretty miserable. The sky was gray. The wind was chilly. And a persistent drizzle fell hour after hour.

"The Christian rock band that was to perform at the rally arrived early, visibly upset by the rain.

" 'We can't rehearse in weather like this!' complained the leader. 'And if we can't rehearse, we won't play. And that's final!'

"Fortunately, Jack Scott was in his best problem-solving mode that day. 'Can't we find a location for your band under cover?' he asked. 'How about the auditorium?'

"Jack led the band over to see the auditorium.

" 'No way,' said the band, barely giving the place a second look. 'It's not nearly big enough, and the acoustics will be terrible.'

"Jack wouldn't give up. 'How about the covered area by the Administration Building — the place where the Jesus statue is?'

"Even before the band got to that area, Jack could tell they weren't thrilled with that prospect, either.

" 'Oh, this won't work at all!' they insisted, and started to turn away.

" 'Why not?' asked Jack. 'There's as much space for your equipment here as you would have out in the open. At least you would be protected even if the campers weren't.'

"The band remained adamant, repeating again and again, 'It just won't work. It just won't work, that's all.'

"Jack, a bit exasperated by this time, demanded to know exactly why that particular spot would not work.

"At last the band leader blurted, 'We can't play around that statue of Jesus. He'd be right in the middle of things!'

" 'You mean,' asked Jack, slowly eyeing each member of the band, 'Jesus would be in your way ?'

"There was a long, embarrassed silence.

"Just then the rain stopped, the sun came out, and the rock band beat a slow retreat to the site originally allocated for its concert, but not without a few thoughtful glances back at the statue.

There were some who thought the band played particularly well that day."

The Forest is aflame in youth rallies.

Chapter 12

Fun And Humor

The Plain Clothes Bishop

Early during his first year in Indiana, Bishop Woodie White spent a quiet week at Epworth Forest. He stayed in the cottage of Tom and Mary Ellen Frost while they were away.

One day the Bishop put on some old clothes and went out walking. Rev. Bill Kaster happened to meet him and stopped to talk. As was his custom, Bill introduced himself as a United Methodist pastor and mentioned what church he was serving. The Bishop quietly acknowledged the introduction.

The two men had quite a long chat, but not a very revealing one so far as Bill was concerned. Who, he kept wondering, is this guy?

Finally, no longer able to contain his curiosity, Bill blurted, "I'm sorry, but I don't think I caught your name."

Responded Woodie with a broad smile, "I'm your new bishop."

Incidentally, Bishop White later reported that his week
at Epworth Forest was nothing short of "great."

Off The Rack

Rev. Ralph Karstedt recalls overhearing older girls at Institute tell the first timers in no uncertain terms that they must all hang their clothes on clothes racks according to size. "It will make borrowing them so much easier," they explained.

Oops!

Ralph also overheard this in the boys' restroom one sweltering day late in Institute week: "I wouldn't mind washing my face, except I forgot the soap!"

65

Tit for Tat

And here's an anecdote recounted by Rebecca Chance Carrington:

"One Sunday morning I was playing for the community worship service in the auditorium. Rev. Sheldon Duecker was preaching that morning. We had known each other since I was very young. He, like some of the other ministers, would often tease me.

"Suddenly there was a lull in the service. Sheldon looked down on me at the organ and said, 'Rebecca, how about you just playing a little something?'

"I looked back at him and whispered, 'How about you just saying a little something?'

"Fun times!"

On The Waterfront

Slippery Watermelons

In 1957 Chuck Hefley became the highly visible (and audible) Waterfront Director at Epworth Forest. Chuck commanded the beach like a Marine drill sergeant. At least the kids thought so. But many discovered that beneath his gruff exterior lay a compassionate, fun-loving soul.

It was Chuck who initiated the infamous Watermelon Scrambles at Institute. Year after year teams of boys from each cottage lined the edge of the water waiting for Chuck to heave a heavily Vaselined watermelon into the lake. Most of the remaining Instituters tried to be there to cheer on their favorite teams.

Once the watermelon splashed into the water, more than a hundred young men would charge into the lake, hoping by hook or crook to bring the melon out of the water, onto the beach, and ultimately back to their cottages as the trophy of the day.

Of course, the thing was so heavily greased that grabbing it was nearly impossible. And even if someone did manage that, he was sure to meet ferocious interference from scores of hands trying to prevent him from taking it ... anywhere!

At times the melon did not survive in edible form, but Chuck and his crew always had enough ice cold watermelons safely stashed away to make sure the winners got their spoils.

In later years the girls had their own Watermelon Scrambles, during which the warfare could be even more fierce.

Hippy Toes

Rinard Hitchcock, or "Hitchie," as he was better known, never intended to work at Epworth; he simply visited the beach area too often. Eventually he and Hefley became a notorious team — Chuck supervising the piers while Hitchcock worked the beach.

Both men communicated in ways that encouraged unquestioning obedience from youth and adults alike. During the decade of the 1960's our grounds suffered both real and imagined corruptions. Those were known as "hippy days." Folks who had no part in Epworth programming found the grounds to their liking for swimming, mellowing out, and associated activities — especially late at night. Rumors of inappropriate waterfront behavior flew wildly. Something had to be done! Somebody had to take charge! So Hefley and Hitchcock found themselves with duties not only during daylight hours but also as security persons while it was dark.

One night Hitchcock found a young couple at the beach lying on a blanket and covered with a second blanket. No inappropriate activities were observed. However, as he passed them he said, "I'll be coming back past here every little while as long as you're here. When I do, I want to see all twenty toes facing in the same direction." Next time he strolled past they were gone. "Hitchie" just chuckled and continued on his rounds.

The Meanest Guy

Some roads at Epworth Forest belong to the county. During the 1960s it became necessary to make deputy sheriffs of some security guards. One Sunday afternoon Hefley found a man at the beach unloading a grill and a cooler of beer.

"I told him he could neither grill on the beach nor drink beer on our grounds," Chuck later recounted. "The man got very abusive. We went nose to nose for awhile, and I finally told him if he didn't stop arguing, I'd put him in jail. He thought that was ridiculous."

"About that time old "Hitchie" meandered by and gently asked the man what the problem was. The man snorted and swore about being illegally prevented from picnicking on the beach.

"Hitchie told him, 'You better listen. He's the meanest guy I've ever seen. Nobody likes him. In fact I've seen him throw a guy in jail before!'

" 'Are you sure?' the man asked.

" 'Sure I'm sure,' said Hitchcock, 'I live right up there in that cottage and I've watched him all summer. He's as mean as they come!'

"Well, the guy picked up his stuff and packed it in his car, muttering and swearing under his breath the whole time.

"The minute he left, Hitchie and I began laughing and just couldn't stop. We were laughing so hard the tears came down in bunches."

More Than One Way to Fill a Communion Glass

Rev. Darrell Taggart recalls this story:

"One night during my first year as Dean of Institute I got really upset. It was communion night and nearly time for the service to begin. To my horror, I suddenly realized that the communion elements were missing. The empty glasses were there but no juice and no bread. Furthermore there was no sign of the women who were in charge of preparing the elements.

"We had to go ahead with the service, of course, and were well into it when we were suddenly distracted by a lot of noise and confusion outside the auditorium. The women had finally gotten to work preparing the elements, but the solemnity of the communion service was shattered, and I was fuming.

"I said nothing, though. What could I say to my District Superintendent's wife?

"The next year, when I met with this same woman and her committee, I let them all know that preparations for communion were to be made well in advance of the service. Certain that I had made myself absolutely clear, I turned my attention to other matters.

"You can imagine my shock when, barely an hour before the communion service, I discovered nothing but empty communion glasses. Again, no juice, no bread, no women!

"Furious, I hopped in my Plymouth and drove to the drug store in North Webster, where I purchased a hot water bottle. Once back at camp, I quickly cut off the business end of the bottle, sterilized it, and filled it with grape juice. Then I commandeered some youth to place the cups in the communion rails and, with thumb and finger pinching the hot water bottle just right, I began filling each little cup with juice.

"At twenty minutes before worship time the too-long absent women strolled up the hill ... and stopped dead in their tracks.

" 'What are you doing?' shrieked the D. S.'s wife. 'And what on earth are you doing it with?'

"Years later, after I had gotten over my anger and she had gotten over her shock, Mrs. A. Wesley Pugh and I had many good laughs over this incident. But she never let me forget it."

A Watery Initiation

Reverend Bob Glass clearly recalls the first Fort Wayne Simpson group he accompanied to Institute. The year was 1978.

It was near midnight on Sunday, arrival day. Bob was down near the lakefront, listening to the brackish water lap up onto the shore and wondering how that week at Institute might go.

Suddenly he found himself surrounded by a group of his cottagers. Just as suddenly each of his arms and legs was grasped by a husky youth. Then together those four youth lifted him off his feet and began swinging his body back and forth, back and forth.

Adults in the group watched indulgently, playing it cool. "They won't throw him into that filthy water," they said. "It'll never happen."

... It happened! The swinging motion went far, far forward. The release was perfectly timed. Bob's body ascended, then descended in a perfect arc — plop, glug!

"It felt like green jello when I landed," he later said. "But it tasted like foul mud."

From that moment on Pastor Bob had the total acceptance of his youth.

The Phantom Snapping Turtle

We'll leave it to our readers to guess who the teller of this story is:

"When Epworth Heights was being developed into Camp Adventure, lots of us helped. Some of the work was pretty filthy, especially dredging to create a swimming area. We weren't exactly happy campers during that job.

"To make matters worse, we were a bit worried about the wild life we were displacing. Did evicted frogs, turtles, and snakes have an ugly side, we wondered?

"One day the dredge kept getting stuck, either at the mouth or way up in the suction pipe. At one point I was just about to stick my hand deep up into the mouth in an effort to pull out whatever was causing the clog, when Thad, my co-worker, shouted. Watch out! There could be a snapping turtle in there!'

"I jumped back, shivering. Then, mustering all my courage, I gingerly stuck my hand in and started groping around. That specter of a snapping turtle had me spooked, though. Whenever I'd touch anything that moved the slightest bit, I'd flinch and jerk my hand back out. In the end the clog turned out to be nothing more than a mess of slimy weeds, but every time I flinched, Thad laughed hysterically.

"Later there was a clog way up in the suction pipe, and it was Thad's turn to clear it. Payback time! Just as he was about to thrust his hand deep into the pipe, I yelled, 'You better watch out! If that snapping turtle managed to get up that far, he's gonna be a whole lot madder than he would have been down at the mouth.'

"It must have taken Thad five or six tries before he could get up the courage to stick his hand inside far enough to pull out the huge, tangled root that was causing the trouble. I laughed till I almost fell into the watering hole we would later call the Pool of Siloam."

The Forest is aflame in fun times.

Chapter 13

The Future Of Epworth Forest

We started this book with the following statement:

"... Epworth Forest is more than a wooded campground. It is, and has been since its beginning, a forest aflame with the Holy Spirit."

It is that Spirit, embodied in the lives of dedicated, self-sacrificing people past and present, that has made Epworth Forest the unique place it is today. It is that Spirit, embodied in the lives of dedicated, self-sacrificing people of the future, that will continue to make Epworth Forest the unique place it needs to be.

What is the future of Epworth Forest?

This is not a new question. It has haunted the minds of many who have loved Epworth since it began in 1924.

Early leaders could not have foreseen many of today's realities, such as music-enriched rallies of thousands of Christian youth. Our forebears could not imagine the startling changes that are now commonplace. In the same way we cannot see what coming years will unveil.

Epworth Forest's future has always been a highly emotional issue. Partly this is true because those of us old enough to have forsworn birthday cakes with the right number of candles tend to want God to be experienced at Epworth Forest in ways familiar to us.

In 1998 FALEF, the Conference Board of Camps and Conferences, and the property owners came together in a visioning effort. Several sessions have thus far been held and the outcomes appear hopeful.

The best question is not "What is the future of Epworth Forest?" but rather "Will God continue to bless, transform, and speak to those who come here?"

We are certain of God's faithfulness, so we are convinced that stories such as those collected here will continue to occur. Our confidence is ultimately not in human efforts but in our loving God's unfailing mercy and the mysteries of Christ's resourcefulness, and the Spirit's presence in and among us, year after year.

If we are obedient in these ways, Epworth Forest will continue to be truly ...

"A Forest Aflame"

1974-1999
A Quarter Century Of Camping
Structures, Policies, And Decisions

Introduction

In 1968 The United Methodist Church came into being. The merger of The Methodist Church and The Evangelical United Brethren Church forever changed the way camping was seen.

Until merger, Epworth Forest and its offspring, Epworth Heights, were the only camp-grounds in the North Indiana Conference of The Methodist Church. They were greatly impacted by the merger, though not as severely as the five campsites that belonged to the other conferences in the merger.

The Northwest Indiana Conference of The Methodist Church felt an even greater impact on Battleground and Pine Creek, while the EUB Conferences felt such an impact on Oakwood, Lakewood, and Asherwood.

The 1968 merger's newly formed North Indiana Conference owned and operated seven campgrounds. As a result, funding priorities and dealing with staff and volunteers became far more complex and the source of numerous unanticipated problems.

Although many problems of the past quarter-century have successfully been confronted, some still remain and new ones keep arising. Even so the North Indiana Conference camping program has emerged as one of the best and strongest in the nation!

The brief account on these pages does not pretend to track all the important decisions, construction projects, and policy issues of Epworth Forest and Epworth Heights (more recently called Camp Adventure). Although titles have changed somewhat to designate camping's parent body we will use the terminology "Commission on Camps and Conferences" (CCC).

We cannot try to name the hundreds of instrumental leaders who gave generously of time, talent, and soul in the cause of outdoor ministries. To name the heroes and heroines of camping would mean little unless there were also space to describe the issues, struggles, and programs through which they became special "saints." Some of their friends and spouses would call them martyrs more than saints, and perhaps some of them were.

The two largest programs — both before and after merger in 1968 — have been Sr. High Institute and Jr. High Camp Adventure. These names seldom appear in this chronological account because the structures of the CCC have not been known by those names.

The Dean's Task Force has been the major force in operating, evaluating, and maintaining Sr. High Institute at Epworth Forest across all these years. Since it has not been substantially altered, it is almost invisible in the accounts which follow.

> Abbreviations: CCC (Commission on Camps & Conferences or Bd of C & C); EF (Epworth Forest); NIC (North Indiana Conference); CA (Camp Adventure)

The Year Before Merger Was A Big Year

1968

In 1967, before merger, two groups supervised program, buildings, and equipment: The Conference Board of Education and Epworth Forest Board. The latter board reported extensive accomplishments in 1967-68.

- Eddie Overmyer — honored for 20 years as Executive Director.
- 1st full-time food service manager hired.
- New swimming pool at Epworth Heights revolutionized Jr. High Camp Adventure.
- 4 new classrooms built near Moore Hall (old Boyville) at Epworth Forest.
- Additional classrooms added to Pell Lodge and Pell Lodge's open shelters were enclosed.
- Big improvements made at Klein Island.
- Craft Hall and the old "slave quarters" razed.
- Hospital moved and enlarged.
- Cafeteria (in hotel basement) wood paneled and new windows installed.
- Front of auditorium and stage remodeled to support more drama.
- Rev. Robert Glass was Executive Secretary, Board of Education.
- Rev. Chuck Johnson was Associate Executive Secretary, Board of Education.

1969

- Ad Hoc Committee on Camping plans 1969 summer program.
- Revised structure: Division on Christian Nurture's Section on Camps and Conferences operated 7 campgrounds: Camp Asherwood
Battle Ground Camp
Epworth Forest
Epworth Heights
Camp Lakewood

Oakwood Park
Pine Creek Camp
- Staff realigned — Rev. Charles Johnson named Associate Director of Conference. Council on Ministries for education and camping.
- Hard work. Major turmoil. The four former conferences got along well!

1970

- 1970 Conference approved study of program and facilities (called by the name of the consulting firm: *BONE, BRITTEN, AND WRIGHT REPORT*). Every camping decision for the next 15 - 20 years bore the imprint of this report.
- Comprehensive statement of philosophy, goals, and purposes requested by Conference.
- Attendance was down.
- Conference authorized the Division of Property and Legal Services to investigate selling Battleground campground.
- Conference approved purchase of 80 acres adjacent to Epworth Heights for $43,000.

1971

- Approved a 10-page statement: "Philosophy for Christian Camps and Conferences for the North Indiana United Methodist Church" as 1970 Conference requested. Rev. Sheldon Duecker directed the process leading to this watershed document, but numerous camping leaders spent thousands of hours on the study and the report. Rev. Charles Johnson was the Conference Resource Staff Specialist giving supervision.
- Conference adopted *BONE, BRITTEN, AND WRIGHT REPORT*
- After heated debate Conference discontinued Asherwood and Battleground and made them available for lease, rent, or sale.
- Hot issue was outsiders coming onto Epworth Forest grounds, interfering with programs and destroying property. Division of Property mandated to solve this problem.

- 3,335 in Sr.. High Institute was the largest attendance in United Methodism nationwide!

- 6,236 total camping participants 3rd largest in North Central Jurisdiction!

1972
- Properties owned by Epworth Forest Foundation were transferred to the Conference.

1973
- Institute Long Range Planning Task Force was inaugurated.

1974
- Eddie Overmyer, Executive Director for 26 years, retires.
- "The Fence" went up around the beach area to maintain security and keep outsiders from troubling campers and programs.

1975
- John Pruett named Director/Manager of Epworth Forest.
- Purchased 35 acres connecting Epworth Forest with Epworth Hills.

1976
- Grandin Godley named General Camp Manager at $1 per year.
- 3% increased attendance after years of decline.
- Leadership Task Force developed guidelines for certifying counselors and directors.
- Boating moved from lakefront to lagoon.
- Full-time employees granted Health Insurance and Pension privileges.
- Mr. and Mrs. Ralph Haynes retired as Camp Adventure Director/Manager after 7 years.

1977
- Bone, Britten, and Wright Report Revised by Commission on Camps and Conferences.
- Cafeteria was remodeled.
- MADD Camp begun: Music, Art, Drama, and Interpretive Dance.
- Epworth Forest scheduled year-round, Epworth Heights from late spring to early fall.
- 15 counselors certified under newly adopted guidelines.
- Alumni and property owners began major tree planting to reforest Epworth Forest.

1980
- Marina built at Epworth Forest.
- North Shore Public Utility connected to North Webster for sewage treatment.
- Camp Adventure new Director/Managers: Jan and Gerry Moser.
- 10 counselors certified; total now 37!
- Swimming pool lighted at Camp Adventure.
- Camp Re-Yo-Ad doubled since 1970 beginning; Deaf Camp tripled since 1976 beginning.

1981
- 4,045 persons attended 56 CCC sponsored events, an increase.
- 14,099 persons attended 425 events not sponsored by the CCC.
- Total of certified counselors = 46, plus 4 camp directors certified.
- 364 work campers worked 3,205 total hours valued at $6,563, plus cash donations of $2,689. Work camps had become crucial to building maintenance.
- Epworth Forest deficit balance: $102,759 in 1976, reduced to $28,651 by 1980, and reduced to $12,105 by 1981.
- Commission on Camps and Conferences reorganized into new Sections and made Interim Report on camping to the 1981 Conference.

1982

- Conference adopted revised philosophy of camping reflecting the "development of Christian faith and discipleship" of the General Board of Discipleship, Division of Education.
- 6 counselors certified.
- 253 camperships awarded.
- Office built at Camp Adventure, a new well dug, and plumbing expanded.
- Final report of Camp Study Task Force completed and adopted by Conference.
- Change name from Special Education Camp to Camp Re-Yo-Ad.
- Summer Sunday Worship averaged 208, summer total of 2,711.
- Epworth Forest trash dump is closed; too much received to maintain it.

1983

- Rev. Chuck Johnson appointed from COM Associate Director to Logansport District Superintendent after serving as camping staff for 17 years.
- Attendance figures showed increase.
- Beginning in 1984 all camp programs but Re-Yo-Ad to operate on registration fees.
- Total camp property valued at $5,000,000.
- Emergency noted — need new roofs on 21 buildings at Camp Adventure.
- As of 1-1-1984 all CCC employees became North Indiana Conference employees.
- "The Fence" around the beach area taken down; few lamented its removal.
- George and Martha McDermott retired after leading Re-Yo-Ad 17 years. It had grown from 20 in 1967 to 197 campers in 1983.
- Grandin Godley resigned as General Manager of Camps.

1984

- 4,685 persons registered for CCC sponsored events in 1983, an increase of 16%.
- 32,247 total Camper Days (3 meals and an overnight). This includes Camper Days at non-CCC sponsored events.
- 43 work camps, 783 workers, 7,712 worker hours, $6,500 value of work.
- 7 counselors certified and 1 camp director. Total now 56 counselors, 7 camp directors.
- Kathy Trotter named 1st Director of Outdoor Ministries, position newly defined and recommended by Camp Study TF.
- CCC requested major funding increase to $216,442 (increase of $56,443).
- Futures' study estimates needs at 5 sites to be $2,900,000.

1985

- 4,536 persons at 60 CCC sponsored events highest in North Central Jurisdiction, though NIC membership was only 5th in the Jurisdiction. Total of 31,239 Camper Days.
- 34 work camps, 4,800 worker hours, cash and in-kind value of $11,410.
- Over 1,700 at Institutes and Bible Conference.
- Scope of site managers' work was enlarged to include programming. One result was the resignation of Jan and Gerry Moser from EF; Dave Marty named new Manager.
- Epworth Forest deficit escalated by $21,578 to $76,126; staff reduced.
- Worship Caravan initiated: 4 days training at EF followed by 1 week touring churches.
- Jeff Pensinger named Director/Manager at CA; 1984 deficit $14,170.

1986

- Jodie Pensinger replaced husband as CA Director/Manager.
- All 5 sites operated with balanced budgets.
- Established Task Force to study and evaluate Sr. High Institute.

- 5 certified as counselors.
- Work began on the Development Project Team of the Capital Funding Committee, a "very exhaustive study."
- Bible Conference (124 youth, 21 staff) held at EF.

1987

- At 5 sites a total of 26,000 participants, 500+ events, and 40,000+ user days.
- 1,000+ volunteers helped at CCC sponsored events.
- Operations and Development Section of CCC was created.
- Finalized and received Master Plan from Camps, Conferences, and Retreats Development Project Team. Presented Master Site Plan to Conference Capital Funds Committee.
- Revised Constitution of Epworth Forest Conference Center approved by Conference.

1988

- Conference adopted CCC Master Site Plan and authorized further work.
- Kathy Trotter, Director of Outdoor Ministries, resigned.
- Steve Anderson named new Director.

1989

- Conference approved "Step into the Future" Capital Funds drive for $6,300,000 for five campsites. $3,487,000 targeted for EF and CA.
- Continued work on Conference-adopted Master Site Plan.
- New soft water system installed at Epworth Forest.
- Brian Scott new Director/Manager at CA.
- Grace Nunery and Joyce Smith honored for many years service in deaf camping.
- Mike Bennett named new director of Re-Yo-Ad.
- Fire destroyed Lookout Lodge at CA.

Step Into The Future —
Capital Funds Campaign

Bishop Leroy C. Hodapp
J. Roberts Dailey, General Campaign Chairman
Dr. Mark Blaising, Clergy Chairman
Welcome Weaver, Challenge Gifts Chairman
Executive Committee of 36

The Campaign was launched following approval at the 1989 Conference session. An 18-page supplement appeared in the Hoosier United Methodist in December of 1989. Rallies were held in all ten districts in January of 1990. The Campaign was rigorously promoted in every phase.

The Campaign failed to reach several of its goals, though many needed maintenance and building projects were completed. Many excellent work camps helped to maximize the work accomplished at the five sites using available funds. However, none of the projected major building projects at Epworth Forest were funded .

The Campaign Committee report to the 1992 annual conference showed pledges of $3,498,898 and $1,283,711 cash received. 478 churches had made some payment to the Campaign while 128 had not.

As funds became available the Step Into the Future Building Committee made allocations to projects by priorities previously established.

In the summer of 1991 a cash flow problem arose. Projects had been undertaken because several large work camp teams were ready, but funds arrived more slowly than anticipated. By late fall the problem abated, and funds began to accumulate for work planned for the following summer.

The 1993 conference extended the deadline for paying pledges from Dec. 31 of 1993 to Dec. 31, 1994, hoping to receive more of the pledged funds.

The 1994 report of the campaign's Building Committee lists projects funded at each site. Camp Adventure had received

$65,761.39 for the new Manager's House and a waste water treatment septic tank and leach field.

That report showed Epworth Forest had received $373,436.31. It was used to remodel North Star lodge and make the following major improvements to each "major lodge" — new insulated roof, new insulated replacement windows, new fluorescent lights, new heating plant, new stucco exterior, floors newly carpeted, bath walls and floors painted, new ventilation, interior painted, new electric substation, and new underground electric service. For the handicapped new sidewalks were built and a restroom was created in two major lodges. Finally, a new maintenance building was built.

1990

- 12.2% increase in user days at 5 camps.
- Completed update on Operational and Policy Guidebook.
- Developed Racial Equality Action Plan (REAP) for Camps and Conferences.
- CCC and Capital Funds Building Committee develop project priority lists for all 5 sites for allocating funds received from the Capital Funds Campaign.
- New "Lookout Lodge" and Manager's House under construction at Camp Adventure.
- Elkhart District Work Camp is primary builder of the new Manager's House!

1991

- New "Lookout Lodge" at Camp Adventure dedicated January 12. Housing for forty has been added to the Lodge, funded through insurance and CCC funds.
- Dave Marty resigns after 7 good years, and in April Keith Vencil becomes new Director of Conference Centers for both Epworth Forest and Oakwood.
- CCC restructured: Epworth Forest Board, Oakwood Center Board, and the former sections of Operations & Development and Publicity gathered into a new Operations Div. of CCC.

- Eddie Overmyer, Executive Director of Epworth Forest for 26 years, died. In his honor the central office building was named "Overmyer Hall."
- "Blue Ribbon Committee" named to consider best models for future Institutes.
- 5 certified as counselors.

1992

- New CCC structure is diagrammed in report to Conference.
- "Step Into the Future" Capital Funds money being used for construction projects.
- Steve Anderson resigns as Director of Outdoor Ministries this spring. In the summer, Dave Arnold, a former leader in CCC, became the new Director.

1993

- New 1992 structure implemented and refined.
- Fiscal 1992 ended with a small surplus after two years of deficits.

1994

- Fiscal 1993 ended with small program and operating surplus.
- Racial Equality Action Plan received emphasis.
- 2-3% increase in attendance overall.

1995

- Fiscal 1994 ended with small program and operating surplus.
- CCC recommends Capital Funds Building Committee continue one more year.
- 9% decrease in overall attendance.

1996

- Final report of Capital Funds Campaign showed $40,000 allocated for remodeling Freeland House, Epworth Forest Hotel.
- Friends and Alumni of Epworth Forest (FALEF) undertook major rebuilding of Freeland House. Phase One: a ground-floor addition to the dining hall plus rest rooms.

- At Camp Adventure Lookout Lodge's heating system modified to burn both gas and wood. Air conditioning being installed.
- Two Pell Lodge classrooms insulated.
- Small increase in attendance reported, 2%.

The Renovation Of
Historic Freeland House Hotel
At Epworth Forest

By
Friends And Alumni Of Epworth Forest (FALEF)

This ambitious campaign officially began Sept. 24, 1996, at a campaign dinner at the Fort Wayne Country Club. Pledges were sought from each guest.

The substantial rebuilding of the 1924-built hotel was first projected at $388,472. Later projections set the need at $600,000.

Phase I extended the dining area beyond the hotel's north wall. After construction, the total dining area expanded to 1,750 square feet, large enough to seat 300 for meals. Restrooms were part of the new construction.

Phase II remodeled the front lobby and all guest rooms on the two floors above the dining area. Interior walls were removed and new ones built in a design with a restroom/shower in each room. There is new wiring and plumbing throughout these floors. All new windows, an air conditioner in each room, a total building sprinkler system, new roof, new vinyl siding, and a new front entrance and deck were all part of this phase. Several rooms were specially designed for handicapped people.

Freeland House has become a brand new guest house with state-of-the-art facilities that meet all modern codes for safety and reliability.

Many people worked long and hard to overcome major obstacles and bring this project to success. Rev. Bob Glass, FALEF President and energetic and persistent leader, was one of the foremost.

"Brother Clyde" Trumbauer was the indefatigable construction boss over the other volunteer construction bosses, who in turn headed up work camps of young and old alike. The faithful "old" workcampers from Elkhart/Michiana again came down in full force. Nearly the entire undertaking was done with volunteers.

The gravely challenging fund raising campaign was led by Chuck Hefley. There are simply too many other officers and faithful soldiers of the campaign to list here, but we and all other lovers of Epworth Forest gratefully salute them all.

Special excitement has come from the fact that 10% of all gifts to help renovate Freeland House are being sent to help finish the construction of Nyembo Christian Center in the Congo. (See earlier story about John Enright.)

1997

- Four sites spent $169,503 on maintenance and improvements, of which $128,766 came from apportionment dollars.
- CCC survey saw $500,000 needed annually for capital and maintenance of four sites plus 5-year needs for improvements of $2,510,000.
- CCC sponsored two listening sessions on racial equality planning in camping.
- Camper database initiated by CCC to enable tracking each individual camper.
- FALEF built new addition to North end of existing dining room at Freeland House.

1998

- Summer attendance up 14.66% — 406 more campers!
- $19,220 awarded in camp scholarships, thanks to Bishop's Christmas Offering.
- Brian Scott resigned as Director/Manager at Camp Adventure.
- T. Scott Greene named Director of Marketing and Publicity.
- Vision Task Force to evaluate CCC ministries and prepare for the new century.
- www.extremecamp.org — became the Email address for CCC camping program.

- Keith Vencil resigned in November as Epworth Forest Manager.
- New dining addition to Freeland House used during summer.
- West side of Freeland House, both floors, totally reconstructed: new interior walls, new windows, restroom & shower in every room, new electric service, new plumbing, sprinkler system. Handicapped accessible.
- T. Scott Greene named Director/Manager of Camp Adventure.

1999

- Summer attendance up over 33% over past two years — 1,000 new campers! Jr. High camping up 45%; Sr.. High Institute up 11%; Bible Conference up 44% !
- Shane Hartman named interim Manager at Epworth Forest.
- $16,400 awarded in camp scholarships.
- Ethnic participation in camping rises to 3.3% of campers.
- East side of Freeland House, both floors, being totally reconstructed: new interior walls, new windows, restroom & shower in every room, new electric service, new plumbing, sprinkler system, and new roof. Reconstructed lobby and entrance deck. Entire building handicapped accessible.
- CCC requested and received from Conference permission to solicit funds from churches, individuals, and agencies of the North Indiana Conference for its Camp Maintenance and Improvements from July 1, 1999, until Dec. 31, 2002.

Closing Note

Those close to the camping program will quickly know how much has been left out of this sketchy chronology. One can easily drown in the facts and records of the camping program. It is so voluminous that very few persons have any grasp of its complexity or extent.

Thousands of volunteers of every age, laity and clergy, women and men, have given themselves unsparing to one or more event or program. Often their service has been repeated year after year. These thousands seem not to have considered the hundreds of miles they drove or the days, weeks, months, and years they spent too high a cost to serve God in camping. We honor them.

Auditorium, dedicated 1924

Cokesbury Inn
Bookstore, gift shop & snack bar above
Changing rooms & waterfront storage below

Freeland House

Chapel, skylighted
Used by small groups & individuals

Lakefront pulpit, early year's Morning Watch site
Restored 1998 in memory of Patricia Hewitt Kline

Camp Adventure's New Lookout Lodge

Thorwaldsen's Christ statue, marble reproduction

Christ statue being washed by youth work camp

Institute Scenes

Institute Youth
What the Keynoter sees

Commitment Night
Nailing covenant promises to cross

Nyembo Christian Conference Center
Enrights Build New Epworth Forest in the Congo

Institute Scenes

Pure joy

Leaving Institute to go back home

Morning Watch in the amphitheater

Cottage counselors are very important people

Good friends are made

Christians smile alot at Institute

Institute Scenes

Pyramid of togetherness

Youth gather at the intersection

Swimming and so much more

Many games of competition

Sailboating from the harbor

Choir School dress rehearsal

Youth Rallies draw large crowds

UMW School of Christian Mission
brings global mission perspective

Elderhostels keep adults young

Many Epworth Forest romances have
become Epworth Forest weddings

FALEF Renovates Freeland House Hotel
1998-99

RV's of work campers parked behind hotel

All new windows and air conditioning

Hundreds volunteer for work camps

All interior walls removed
New walls create new floor plans

New shower stalls fit through window openings

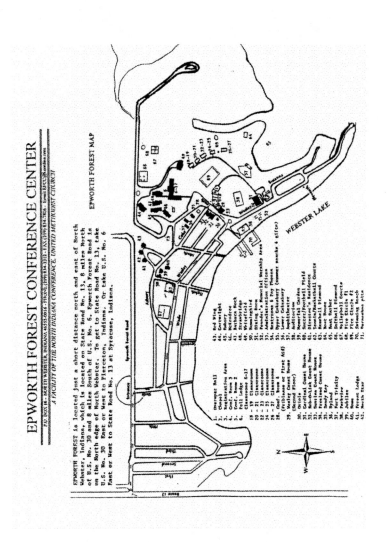

Epworth Forest grounds and facilities

Everywhere children need
to, in the darkness of their disabilities,
They wait, and knowing they will
to be found, to be helped, to be taught.

The Indiana Department of Public Instruction
awards this

CERTIFICATE of APPRECIATION

to

Epworth Forrest United Methodist Camp

North Webster

A special child has a special opportunity today because of your efforts on behalf of the Search for Special Children. Though that knowledge alone is a much higher recognition than any document can render, this certificate is presented as a small token of our gratitude. Your individual participation, multiplied by the participation of many others, resulted in a successful statewide program to provide handicapped children with the Special Education that will help them live full, valuable lives. Spring, 1976

Superintendent
Department of Public Instruction

Director
Division of Special Education

Indiana Dept. of Public Instruction Award

Index

Acknowledgments

It is only fitting that we should endeavor to acknowledge the scores of people who contributed, either directly or indirectly, to the writing of this book.

First of all, there were those who contributed stories. These included people interviewed in person, by letter, by phone, and on tape. Although we could include only a small portion of their stories in this book, we read and appreciated every one. All helped to mold the character of this book. And once this book is printed, all stories will be sent to the United Methodist archives at DePauw, so none will be lost.

Secondly, there were those who submitted important records. These ranged all the way from back issues of *Conference Journals* (thank you, Jim and Jo Babbitt), to files loaned by persons in charge of specific programs, to tons of files loaned by the Conference staff in Marion, to tons of files loaned by the office at Epworth Forest. Thank you, Rosie Tucker and Conference office staff, Keith and Laura Vencil, Shane Hartman, and various support persons.

Then there were those who contributed pictures. The staffs at Epworth Forest and Camp Adventure were particularly helpful in this respect. But there were private parties, too, who shared their photos. Again, we could not begin to include all of those pictures in the book, but we enjoyed the privilege of viewing them. Like the personal stories, those pictures helped to mold the character of this book.

Finally, there were those who provided the motivation to write this book. Most particularly, we want to thank Bob Glass and the rest of the FALEF board for first commissioning the book and then encouraging us along the way. Admittedly, there were times when the job seemed just too formidable, just too overwhelming, even just plain impossible! But Bob Glass is the Gentle Persuader, if ever anyone was worthy of that name. In the end, it was his continued interest in the project, his conviction that we could do it, and a deadline that loomed ever more threateningly that got the job done.

Abundant thanks to you all!

John and Joyce Elliott